Pascalune HD

From Homo Sapiens
to Homo Deus

How to complete Man's evolution?

A practical guide

© 2020 Pascalune HD.
Publication date: June 2020.
ISBN: 9782322222520
BoD-Books on Demand
12-14 rond-point des Champs-Élysées, 75008 Paris
Printed: Books on Demand, Norderstedt, Allemagne

To my seven billion selves.

We are all **connected**.
If I evolve, everything evolves.
If I evolve, Humanity evolves.
If I evolve, the Universe evolves.
It is useless and vain to expect someone else
to accomplish this work at my place.

We are here on earth to live out the Awakening:
an awakening to one's true divine nature
beyond the shadows of this illusory world.

Translated from the French: **Laurent Thompson.**

Cover: **Martin Trystram.**

The basis of a successful education for our children is to apply the principle of non-intervention as much as possible. Thus the child can experiment himself the actions leading to success versus a longer and more fastidious way.
Non-intervention by the parent is a token of love, of trust in his child's ability to succeed.
To gather one's own experience is the unique manner to understand and evolve.
The same goes for us, human beings who have come on this planet to grow in wisdom and conscience.

There isn't on the one hand the Creator and on the other me, his creature. No, I am the Creator AND the creature. Separation is an illusion brought on by this apparently dual world. Unity is the only reality.
I create my own experiences on this planet.

When we know, beyond the shadow of a doubt, that we are the great Consciousness in the process of experimenting itself, Homo Deus may be incarnated in matter because we behave each day in the light of this unshakeable knowledge. This is reflected in our thoughts, in our words and actions.
Thus, the elements that are needed to complete our evolution are anchored in our present moment and the metamorphosis may take place!

It is enough for one human to pass on to the next stage beyond Homo Sapiens to prove that Homo Deus is possible. These precursors can open a new path to follow.
And…good news, many humans have already brilliantly done so!
I name: Buddha, Jesus Christ, Bhaisajyaguru, Amitabha and many more lesser known.

Two thousand years ago, the teaching which enabled one to manifest his own divine nature was reserved to only a few initiates…Nowadays however, thanks to the rising vibration of this planet and the mass awakening to consciousness, the Homo Deus evolution is open to all!
First of all, this teaching is within each and everyone's grasp. It took me only several years of intuitive listening, of inner guidance, discernment and research to conceive the essence of this knowledge.
Anyone can therefore access it to his convenience, as long as he sets his heart to it.
Secondly, it's application in day to day living in terms of an absolute incarnation of the divine version (Homo Deus), here and now, in our own body of flesh, has become reality to whomever is fervently dedicated to it.
Around us, everything is auspicious for this human revolution. Including global warming and freedom-destroying laws which current governments are aiming to put in place.
So, let's hop on the moving train and jump with both feet into this marvelous adventure which is the new paradigm!

A potent energy has created the universe and the world as we perceive it. This is a fact.
So what kind of energy is it?
It's interesting to know the basic nature of this primal energy because it will thereby enable us to grasp the energy which is to remain throughout all of the 'material' experience.
Let's think logically, which type of energy could well have conceived matter in this universe? Could it have been the energy of hate? Or of fear? Or the energy of Love?
The energy of hate is destruction. That of fear is separation. These two energies disunite that which is whole, they disassemble what is combined.
The original energy is one which unites, engenders and creates. Only Love unites. Love engenders and Love creates.

So Love has begotten everything. Including hate and fear…
To which purpose? In order to experiment death, separation, dissociation, war, destruction. In other words, to experiment exactly that which it isn't.
Love longs to create that which it isn't in order to 'become aware' of that which it is.
Without shadow, we don't perceive what is light.
Without separation, we can't understand what union is.
Without death, we can't conceive what life is.
Without war, we don't grasp what is peace.
Without selfishness, we can't recognize what generosity is…

To conclude, everything springs from Love and everything returns to it.

**Today, in 2020, the time has come to incarnate this divine energy found in each one of us.
Let us become Homo Deus.**

We are waited upon during this period of planetary ascension in which each and every one has the possibility to become the most divine version of his/her self!

You may have thought that the evolution of Homo Sapiens had reached it's term?
Not so. Our evolution is still in progress…
Soon, human beings shall enter an infinitely more majestic phase having as sole guide, Love, with the daily understanding and living out of our true nature.

The result is guaranteed if you fully and totally integrate each of the forty steps.
Goal attained in forty steps.

Take enough time to assimilate and live out each teaching. One day, three days, a month, a year or a lifetime? It doesn't matter, you are your own master.
The fact alone of wanting to follow this particular and bold path is in of itself already an accomplishment.

Nowadays, there aren't any more mysteries nor secrets left on how to become a Homo Deus. This book is a token of this.
Nonetheless, the difficulty resides in following the forty steps in full conscience, to feel them as deeply right and perfect for you, to doubt no longer and to become a pure incarnation of Love consciousness.
This is the real challenge…

The order of the forty steps is a suggestion and in no case an obligation.
You can learn and integrate them in the order which suits you best, the result will be the same.

Time has come to recall your true nature and to manifest it daily.
The hour has come to place yourself back in the center of your life, to fully assume responsibility and sovereignty over it.
Cease handing to others your power, your freedom or your security.
Beyond all appearances, only you are to deal with it.

This book shall lead you on the path to your freedom, at ALL times and in ALL areas.

STEP 1

The unique unwavering certainty is that your conscience exists.

Only your conscience exists.
If you question all knowledge in order to forge your own based on one absolute certainty. The only reality which holds is that you are in the process of thinking.
All the rest may be a dream, an illusion, a theater setting or a 'matrix' mirroring to you a virtual world…

You may be certain of only one thing: *"you think, therefore you are."*
As Rene Descartes said and before him, Gomez Pereira, the philosopher:
    "I think therefore I am".
    "I am inasmuch as I think".

If your conscience is your only reality, you can measure all the power of the present moment!
Thus, only trust the present moment, because it's the only moment in which you fully are. In the final analysis, this infinity of succeeding present moments represents the best way to influence in concrete terms your existence. Act now and cease putting off to tomorrow what you can do right away.

Lay your attention on your body, on the emotions running through you, on the sensations which your five senses are relaying to you.

That alone is your reality!
Forget the past.
Forget the future.
Live only in the present.
Understand that only the present exists. You never were in the past, nor ever will be in the future. You are continuously in ONE present time. Always the same present which lasts and goes on indefinitely. This present is permanent! You may stop relating this present to a past or a future. This present exists in an omnipresent fashion! The present IS. Because only that is, before, during and after. ALWAYS.
Be joyous now. Remain present.

As soon as you are invaded by your thoughts, as soon as you realize that you are invaded by your thoughts, then repeat, mentally or out loud, the word: 'Now.'

At each moment of the day, repeat or think on the word 'Now'.
When you go to bed, start again to murmur or think: 'Now'.
Slowly pronounce this word to grasp it's full meaning. It's powerful: NOW... NOW...NOW

Remain present. Be present to yourself.
NOW, focus your attention on what's going on around you, on what your skin is touching, your nose smells, your ears hear, your eyes see...
This exercise will free you from anguish over the future, from remorse and regrets over the past.

Repeat this word each time you want to recover calmness. Because in reality, in the present time, everything often goes very well! Only your imagination feeds your fear by hatching catastrophic scenarios.

For a moment, consider yourself as a caterpillar.
This book and the integration of the forty steps represent the chrysalis period.
Following this encounter with yourself, with your true nature, with a yet unknown reality that you are about to touch with your fingertips, shall emerge the butterfly that was still dormant in you!
Welcome to this experience rich in learning that you have chosen to live NOW.

The release of doubt on what is real and what isn't.
The release of all endless questioning
because only one thing is sure:
You think, you are,
therefore your conscience exists.
YOU ARE EVERYTHING.

STEP 2

Look at yourself lovingly. Love yourself.

Observe your body in a mirror.
What your eyes of flesh see is your physical appearance, in other words, a facet of yourself. On the other hand, what you see in a reflection isn't your deep and true nature. You own many facets but eyes of flesh can only see bodies of flesh.

If you don't love yourself, why would others love you?
If you don't love yourself, how could you love others?
If you don't accept your faults, your weaknesses and your imperfections, how could you accept those of others?
Look at yourself without judging. Ignore the dictates of beauty imposed on us by our society.
Love the color of your skin, love the width of your hips, love your hair, love the size of your body, of your penis or of your breasts, love your hairiness, love the shape of your nose, love the particularities which make up your physical appearance.

Free yourself from the need of having someone else admire or compliment you.
Do you want to hear soft words or expressions of love? Tell them to yourself and receive the compliments with gratitude.

Stop denaturing your body to please others.
Stop wanting to get thinner, or fatter, to tweeze yourself, shave, or put on makeup…for the unique purpose of wanting to please others.
Do it only if it provides you with real joy. Be honest with yourself to know whether you are doing it for you or out of social pressure.

Love your body, regardless of its state, age or health. It's here today with you and for you. It's your indivisible team mate through your life on earth. Make the most of it and thank it!
Without it you couldn't have lived the experiences you had nor those that you will have. Without it, you would be in the state of a disincarnate soul. To be a soul without a body, has its advantages but doesn't imply the same effort or work, in this state you can't evolve!
On earth where duality reigns, your training is exacerbated and highly efficient. Because here, all is made for you to grow in conscience.
Every passage on this earth is at the outset a success, a victory over yourself.
What is after death won't allow you to pursue the evolution of your conscience.
Everything is played here and now.
So thank yourself for having accepted this bold challenge!
Because, even if you have no remembrance of it, you validated this incarnation. Free will is total and universal.
Had you said 'no' to this existence, you wouldn't have been born.
However, you are here.

You may trust yourself. Your soul aptly knows what it has programmed in order to evolve.
Listen and follow its precious advice, it shall transform your life.

You 'integrated' your body a number of years ago. You may be certain of this: your body loves you.
It's doing its best in the given conditions. Thus, love it with unconditional love.
Cuddle your own body, massage it, caress it, take care of it, hydrate it and feed it with healthy and varied food.
Look up the benefits of different food. Favor fruits and vegetables that are fresh, raw, seasonal, local and without pesticides.
Shut the television off because it gives the floor to individuals who are disconnected from reality and from their humanity. They propagate deceptive advice sponsored by numerous lobbies.
Think by yourself.
Seek information by listening and following your intuition and discernment.
Discover new recipes and superfoods (spirulina, chlorella, chia seeds, maca, curcuma, ginger, garlic…), try new ingredients, the earth is so bountiful!

Release of your need to be loved and desired.
Release of your need to please others
and to fit within the norms of society.
Release of the burden of what others may think.
YOU ARE EVERYTHING.

STEP 3

Become a vegetarian.
The 'Source' is one unique conscience
experimenting an infinity of facets.
Therefore, I am the other and the other is me.

You are the other.
You are the smallest. But you are also the greatest. As all the rest!
In spite of appearances, you are human but you are also the horse, the pig, the butterfly, the tree, water,…
In order for our soul to evolve in conscience, we must apply change at all levels of our being by working on our thoughts, our speech and our actions.
If the change is only in the mind, at the level of thought or even speech, it won't be enough to make roots in our everyday lives.

Little by little, start removing meat and fish from your diet. Suffer no more harming others to feed yourself. You don't need to anymore. In the west, nowadays, vegetable proteins may be found everywhere. Chick peas, red beans, lentils in all colors, sprouted seeds, spinach, kale cabbage,…
These plants are rich in protein and iron. In addition, they are more easily digestible than animal protein.
Vegetables and dried vegetables are cheaper than meat, even when choosing organic and local producers!

Moreover, you are fed by the love you give to other beings, to plants, to yourself, to the universe, to the Great All.

Follow your yearnings. If you wish to reduce your meat consumption, help yourself by finding new vegetarian recipes and new ingredients which will insure the nutritive intake of protein.
Inform yourself on the actual consequences of a meat diet on the human body. Bear in mind that there exists an "animal industry lobby". This lobby is paid to hide certain truths from you as long as you continue to fatten them financially while becoming fat…

Beyond these down to earth arguments, know that the vibrational consequences of a meat diet on your bodies (physical, mental and emotional) are not irrelevant.
By consuming a dead animal, what kind of energies are you absorbing?
Energies impregnating a piece of flesh coming from a sentient being who lived a life of torture before an ignominious death.
What benefit can one hope to obtain from this kind of diet? Do you prefer to ingest pieces of corpses having suffered untold misery during their short lives? Or vegetables which have grown in a field, fed with water, sun and earth nutrients?

Let's abide now in the heights of universal conscience beyond 'good and evil', of the 'suffering' or 'wellbeing' of all things.

You are EVERYTHING, you can see yourself in each element.
Thus, listen to yourself and nourish yourself with ingredients which will make you grow and mature in love.

Your new motto is:
"Do to others what you would want others do to you".

Whether it be to the passerby hustling you, to the steak you want to devour, to the child who insists on getting a little attention from you, to the depressed neighbor, to the shelter-less who asks for a bit of money, to this fly trying to exit the room…
Picture yourself in their shoes then act upon that which would seem ideal for you in this situation.

Meat is not necessary for good health. It rather seems to be harmful in view of the industrial quality and exaggerated quantities consumed by humans.
Find out about vegetarian recipes and which vegetable ingredients to choose from in order to replace meat.
Offer yourself a soft dietary transition.
Respect your cravings and don't constrain your body through frustration or rude privation. Accomplish it in a light and fluid manner.

**Release of your need to eat
living and sensitive beings.
YOU ARE EVERYTHING.**

STEP 4

Walk and particularly, walk in nature!

Socrates was a great walker, Rimbaud, Kant and Rousseau too, and so many others as well…
They walked to think, to meditate, to rid their minds of persistent thoughts, to meet people, to discover new landscapes.

This fluid body movement frees the mind.
If moreover you walk in the forest, in the mountains, in the countryside, by the sea, a lake or a river, this will facilitate your connection to the forces of nature.
Your natural environment is outside! It's there to replenish you. You weren't made to live between four walls nor in concrete cities in which the dominating color is grey.
Nature provides energy, joy and well-being.
The more time you spend outdoors, the more your mind will be alert and your body healthy.
Notice that the modern way of life is actually the opposite of what is beneficial to you: walking is swapped with sitting in a car or in front of a desk.
Asphalt roads and buildings replace the blue sky and the countryside.
Animal and insects, which were daily at our side, have been eradicated through the use of pesticides, insecticides and security laws.
Raw foods, local and vegetable were wiped out in favor of junk food originating from the other side of the globe.
And the list is long…

Walking also permits to go out and meet others and to observe the world.
Walking increases creativity. Walking stimulates thought, it eases concentration. It contributes to having a fit body. Contrarily to what one may expect, walking is an ideal remedy for back pain.

Walking is a sort of meditation; it rids your body of an incalculable number of sterile and redundant thoughts. Thus it clears up space in the mind, opening up the way to receive at last some new and inspiring ideas.
Your mind cannot receive an idea properly if it's constantly brooding over a past concern, a future fear or a contained anger…
It must be at peace. Only then will it hear the subtle and discreet idea whispered by your soul.

Ideas emanate from the 'Great All'; they are sent to you when your mind is available to receive them. Your mind is like a radio receiving waves. The human being is like a radio set able to capture high frequencies (but also low frequencies when his mindset is anxious).
Walking helps 'divine reception' because it has your body oxygenate and has you think about other things.

When we have an intuition, this means that we have just received an idea which doesn't come from our mind, nor from our memory nor from our intellectual background.
An intuition originates from beyond our own life experience, it comes from 'The Source', from 'The Great All'.

When a person becomes inspired, this means that she receives an array of intuitions! A burst of intuitive and omniscient knowledge.
We all get ideas. And this happens countless times each day. The difficult part is listening to them and putting them to practice…
Brilliant or commonplace, all ideas are perfect and arrive at the right moment.
The more you can fine tune your perception at the moment of receiving an idea (not your simple thoughts), the more you'll feel a powerful and transcending surge at that very moment!
Soon, whenever a vibrant idea passes through you, you'll feel great spiritual bliss…

**Release of your need to work in a job
which doesn't suit you to 'earn a living'.
Listen to your ideas, they will dictate to you
how to plan your day, little by little.
Be your own boss. Be your own guide.
Be your own compass.
Release of your need to control,
to program, to anticipate.
Trust in yourself, in life, in love,
in your wonderful ideas.
You walk therefore you are.
YOU ARE EVERYTHING.**

STEP 5

Laugh and be joyful.

Joy!
Joyfulness is your basic state.
The other emotions are there to show you that you're following a path which isn't in accordance with your deeper self.
They are 'emotional guides' indicating that you may fully accept what you are living now, in order to find joy again, which is your permanent state.

Learn how to decode the messages sent to you by the four main emotions; your basic emotion, in other words, your basic state, being that of joy.

FEAR:

When you are afraid, this means that **you must act**. If you do nothing, if you persist on this path, you are taking great risks, perhaps even death.
Thus, when fear manifests itself, learn how to regain your senses and to act by listening to the idea of action which naturally comes to your mind.
You act, therefore you recover your personal power and cease to be a helpless victim when problems pop up.
You act, therefore you listen to yourself and become an actor of your life rather than an impotent observer.

SADNESS:

You feel sad when life shows you that **a period is coming to an end**.

Thus, you must mourn before allowing the new period to set in.

Sadness must be welcomed with love and gratitude. Through it you become conscious that certain things are about to change in your daily life and that you are going to have to adapt to an unknown situation.

You trust yourself and have faith in the perfection of life and the wealth of its teachings through which events occur at an ideal moment for your personal growth.

ANGER:

If you are angry, this means that **you need to communicate**!

Anger fills you when your limits are not respected, when you feel denigrated, not respected for who you are.

A situation which seems unfair to you will make you angry.

The solution is to express yourself, to assert yourself. Anger invites you, pushes you, begs you to communicate clearly so that your perspective of things may be heard.

Therefore, someone who is angry has the need to be listened to with consideration, and to be taken seriously.

JOY:

Are you joyful? Keep on that way, **you're on the right track**!

Your attitude and your choices are perfect.

Whenever you lose this joy and find it replaced by one of the three aforementioned emotions, this means that you must reconsider your decisions, change some part in your way of life.

In short, your emotions are precious allies!
Their purpose is not to make your life miserable, unless you don't listen to them and reject the actions which would allow you to find harmony again.
Laugh and smile at any occasion. Take life as a stage play full of surprises, amazing twists and humor!
Notice that when you laugh, you feel light. Everything becomes simple and is an occasion to laugh!
Laughter and joy are 'the keys of Heaven on earth'.
The 'Mona Lisa' painted by Leonardo da Vinci holds a clue to find happiness: She teaches us to smile always.
Don't take things too seriously, quit looking at the world so solemnly…
Because your solemnity won't change anything to the situation. Unless it makes things worse.
On the other hand, your joy and enthusiasm are contagious to those around you as much as to you.
Your smile will lighten up your face and appease your body. This well-being will affect your other subtle bodies (mental and emotional particularly).

When you laugh, your vibration is so much higher!
You feel that you're in expansion, in a symbiosis with the world.
If you don't have the heart to laugh because you identify yourself too much with your 'incarnate persona', then dance, sing, cry out in joy! Play at being euphoric and it will radiate through your cells…

Move what you know how to move in your body and breathe in slowly to oxygenate your lungs.
You are present, here and now. Nothing else matters.

Smile or laugh whenever you can.
Make yourself joyful, this will immediately lighten your thoughts.
You can't control events. However, you can manage your attitude towards these same events! You can alter your reactions, your attitude.
Turn your tears of sorrow into tears of joy.
Welcome lovingly what is and what you cannot change. Then laugh at this awareness, because you're infinitely more than that.
Remember that in reality, only Love exists.
Burst out laughing, play the game entirely.
If necessary, even pretend to laugh to get the ball rolling, doing 'as if' creates the stimulus needed to bring about real laughter, the authentic outburst of laughter.

Thanks to humor, everything can be said. Why? Because laughter allows for a distance to be made from the unpleasant feeling or difficult event. Nothing is worse than to feel stuck in a problem, without any visibility other than the narrow visibility of one's own weak and egotistical self.

Release of your need to be serious and to be taken seriously by your entourage.
Release of your duty to be 'an adult'.
Reunion with your 'inner child'.
YOU ARE EVERYTHING.

STEP 6

Detach yourself from your roles and affiliations.

You are.
You no longer have any names.
No first name, no family name, no birthdate.
Time doesn't exist.
You no longer have any nationality, no identity. You're just a living being among other living beings.
Why does the Universal Conscience 'need' to incarnate itself into a multitude of beings?
Just like you, it yearns to know itself, to express and discover itself.
During your childhood, as soon as you understood that your body belonged to you and that you were free of your time, what did you do?
You straightaway and continuously wanted to experiment your relation to others, as well as to objects, toys, food, nature…
You tasted a multitude of savors in order to determine which ones you liked and those that were less pleasant to your palate.
In your games, you took on a great number of characters:
You were the nice guy, the bad guy, the cowboy, the Indian, the mermaid, the pirate, the baby, the mother, the father, the pupil, the schoolmaster, the warrior, the knight, the poor, the queen, the orphan, the servant, the saint, the hero, the thief, the cheater, the fool, the horse, the bullfighter, the bird…

You disguised yourself. You interpreted those roles in your games, in plays, in videos done alone or with friends...
You wrote horror stories, comedies, sentimental novels, fictions, autobiographies...
You drew with paint, crayons or felt-tips, bright colorful works, and others very dark.
You invented epic frescoes, unusual portraits, imaginary worlds...
You met magnificent beings, and others, which put you in a furious rage or deep sorrow. You discovered your reactions towards these different individuals.
You've loved, adored, adulated, admired.
You've hated, despised, scorned, ignored.
You've felt yourself alive, you've thought yourself dead, you've lived sadness, joy, nostalgia, fear and fury.

This allowed you to learn more about yourself, more intensely and more deeply.
Like you, the Universal Conscience loves to express its thousand and one aspects. It longs to taste itself, revels in being this way and also that way.
Conscience is Love.
On the other hand, it allowed itself to forget this Love, this All, in order to rediscover it again and again.
Forgetting in order to live the ecstasy of discovery. And this, infinitely! To the point of completely incarnating this energy of pure Love in matter, until spiritualizing this matter.

For this step, get into the habit of talking about yourself in the third person. At least in your thoughts and in your mind.

There's no more 'I' because you have returned to be 'ALL'.

You become one of the experiments of the Universal Conscience.

Therefore you speak with distance of 'your' ego, of 'your' mind, of 'your' incarnated physical personality, which isn't your true essence…

For example: "He feels miserable today because he's unemployed. He's afraid not to have enough money to live abundantly."

**Release of your need to put on such or such a role, which is reducing, dividing, unhealthy, constraining.
Release of people's expectations of you because of the part you're supposed to take in society.
YOU ARE EVERYTHING.**

STEP 7

What makes you suffer from the outside comes from pain inside of you.

When you see or hear about an event, which strikes you by its sheer horror, stop wanting to try to change the world and its imperfections. But observe inside of you the wound that it awakes, the fear that it reveals.
The outer world is there to transmute emotions buried inside of you and which you refuse to look at squarely.
We are all ONE. We are all interconnected.
The changes, which you manage to accomplish in you, will inevitably have a repercussion on the rest of humanity.
We are all linked. Separation is only an illusion.

Send love to the events and people, which you find horrible, because if they're in your field of perception that means that their darkness is also a part of you.
Remember that only the Universal Conscience exists. And since you exist then you are this Universal Conscience.
YOUR conscience IS the Universal Conscience. Or rather, the Universal Conscience IS YOUR conscience.
Besides your conscience, you don't have any proof that anything else really exists.
Thus, welcome on board the drama being played through you.
Don't try anymore wanting to change the world, society, others, your partner or your family.
"Be the change which you would like to see in the world" once said Gandhi.

The proverb of 'the straw and the beam' could apply to the whole world!
Explanation: What you reproach to others comes from you. The other is the magnifying glass of the qualities and faults, which you already possess in you.
You are here on earth to experiment what your essence is not in reality:
You are not mortal. You are unchanging, neither born, nor dead. You are outside of time. You are.
You are not made up of any fear, of any hate. Fear and hate only serve you in this incarnation to reveal what you are by opposition. You are pure love.
You are neither separated from others, nor from the rest of the universe. Everything is One. Total UNITY. Therefore there can be no hierarchy because we are all equal.

Thus, there exists no difference between a king and his subject nor between a human and an insect.
We all come from the same creative source; we are all fruits of the Universal Conscience.
We ARE the Universal Conscience.
You need only to obey your own soul, not the law, a boss, a policeman or a teacher...

Thus, there shall be darkness, fear, manipulation, lies on this planet, as long as you perpetuate these in your day-to-day life, in your relations with others.
Even in infinitesimal amounts, even if you're convinced that 'this little lie' or this necessary 'secret' is for the welfare of others.

You shall live hell on earth, as long as you refuse to see that you have shadowy parts to transmute, or keep persuading yourself that you're perfect or superior to others.

Practice each day the 'Ho'oponopono' technique.
As soon as you hate somebody (a corrupted politician, a dishonest president, a rapist film producer, an assassin, an immoral banker, a pedophile, an egocentric star, the new girlfriend of your ex, a narcissistic pervert, a dictator, Satan, the Illuminati…) look at his/her photo and repeat these words:
"I'm sorry. Forgive me. Thank you. I Love you."
You may even pronounce these words in front of the mirror, to your intent.

Release of your need to struggle in order to manage, dominate, appease or hush up your emotions.
Release of the impression to be powerless when facing the horrors of this world, because you are the change that you want to see in this world. Act.
YOU ARE EVERYTHING.

STEP 8

Don't identify yourself to the emotions you feel.

Disunite yourself from them. They are not yours.

Now that you've learned how to decrypt the role of your emotions (as a reminder, refer to step 5), learn to transcend them!
Because on the way that leads to Homo Deus, you no longer identify yourself to the egocentric character that you are still incarnating now. You are beyond that, beyond everything.

Feelings (so called 'positive' or 'negative') tend to monopolize your attention. As soon as you become aware of it, welcome them without judgment.
Don't put any labels on them, neither 'good' nor 'bad', nor even 'pleasant' or 'unpleasant'.
Look at them with goodwill.
Let them pass and smile as you see them emerge, hang on and vanish in you.
You are not your feelings.
You are. Quite simply

Let go of terms like 'I' or 'Me'. Choose to say 'All' or 'It' instead.
So as to discard any identification with yourself, your ego, your human individuality or physical body, replacing the word 'I' by 'It' will ease detachment from your emotions.

Mentally or in a hushed voice describe what is going on inside you in a detached way:
'It's afraid'.
'It feels anger in response to so and so's reaction'.
'It's hungry and it thinks that it must absolutely eat something right away'.
'It likes watching this film'.
'It would sure like to win the lottery'.
'All is experimenting anguish'.
'All is feeling very frustrated'.

Drink some water. Water attenuates the overflow of emotions welled up in you.
It's also advisable to exit the room in which you've lost your temper; the best is to go outside.
Fresh and stimulating air will shortly dissipate your stress.
If you have a surplus of energy to discharge, don't hesitate to go for a walk.
To hike for an hour isn't an obligation, just around the block will do to appease your mind.

If you wish to install de-identification with your ego, you could say: *"Good morning, illusion of 'I'!"* when you wake up first thing in the morning.

As of today, learn to see that what surrounds you is sensitive and endowed with a conscience!

Respect the chair on which you're seated, the PC you work on, the car that you drive, the grass brushing against your feet, the breeze caressing you…

Thank each piece of food you're about to eat and enjoy it conscientiously.
Take time to savor, appreciate and chew it.
Make the most of the instant when the morsel is perceptible to your palate and taste buds because as soon as it's swallowed, you'll lose track of it. As if it had disappeared.
The so-called 'primitive' people thought that each stone, each cloud, each flame or each stream was alive.
North American Indians believed that they were an integral part of this world, without hierarchy and that all are equal.
To them, the butterfly was just as important as the buffalo or the corn.

But the actual awakening of consciences is calling us back towards what is essential. And the mirages of materialism are no longer able to veil our universality.

Have you ever heard of 'The *New Medicine*' of Dr. Ryke Geerd Hamer?
This German doctor has put to light the mechanism of what leads to cancer.
Two months after the premature death of his son, Dr. Hamer discovers that he has a tumor in the testicles.
Intuitively, he links the shock over the loss of his son with the appearance of his cancer.
To understand the process, he studies the brain scans of his cancerous patients.

His analysis reveals that a violent trauma (death of kin, divorce, psychic shock…) will create some alteration of the brain.
This alteration shall be referred to as the 'Hamer foci'. This will eventually give rise to cancer.

Dr Hamer notices that breast cancers result from unresolved conflict between daughter and mother; that cancer of the cervix is due to a problematic relation to sex…
Dr Hamer established the 'Iron Rule of Cancer'. It may be resumed thus:
'Any cancer or equivalent disease starts off with a DHS (Dirk Hamer Syndrom).'
(Dirk was the name of his deceased son).
Indeed, DHS is the shock from a brutal conflict lived in a dramatic way and in isolation.
At the moment of a DHS, a 'Hamer foci' is created at three levels: psychic, cerebral and organic.
The type of conflict will determine the localization of the foci in the brain and in the organ in which the cancer will develop.
From that point on, the cancer will develop in proportion to the evolution of the conflict that isn't dealt with.
What he mostly highlights is the fact that each disease has a very specific reason to appear. The illness is precisely the program, which our body sets up to cure the DHS trauma!
Dr Hamer remarks that germs are not our enemies. On the contrary, they are useful and are involved during the healing process.

It would therefore be counterproductive to eradicate the symptoms through medication, because these symptoms are in fact the key to our future healing…
This is why most animals can heal spontaneously.
It was also the case of humans before they started giving credit to screenings, surgery or chemotherapy.
A person must understand, express, welcome and appease the initial trauma for healing to take place.
Thus it would be so much more useful to go see a psychologist rather than an oncologist…

In fact Dr Hamer doesn't use the term 'disease', he replaces it with more neutral words: 'Special Biological Program".
'Special' because this program is temporary and exceptional with respect to the body's normal living operation.

**Release of your need of having to feel positive or negative emotions to reassure your ego that it's in fact alive or that your life is important.
YOU ARE EVERYTHING.**

STEP 9

You no longer need to think about the past.

No need to keep on analyzing your body to try and penetrate the secret causes of your physical pain, of your blocks, of your past and present illnesses.
You're no longer this body, let it heal itself. As it wants and when it wants.

You just need to love it as it is; to respect the way it operates and manages the traumas and suffering it has had to endure.
Accept what is.
Don't try to understand these traumas, nor to detect their origin.
Let go of the hope of unraveling the mystery of such and such disease that you suffer from.
Let go of old beliefs as well as the insane energy you spend trying to heal wounds of the past.
When you understand that you are NOT the person to whom these difficulties have occurred, then you'll cease to suffer from them. Automatically.
You will become aware that the person reading this book right now isn't really you.
Because you are the 'Universal Conscience' reading through your human eyes in order to experiment this facet of itself.
And this Absolute Conscience reads and lives through each human, each animal, each plant and each element on this earth and in the whole universe!

You don't need to fight 'against' your disease since you aren't really this ill body.
No one is irreplaceable. Nevertheless, each one is unique.
When you integrate the fact that the person acting in this play, is only an infinitesimal part of YOU, therefore of All, then you have no expectations to heal. Everything is perfect as an experience.
If you heal, it's perfect. If you don't, it's also perfect.
EVERYTHING is experience.
Letting go is another key to self-fulfillment.

"Crises, disruptions and disease don't suddenly appear by chance. They are indicators for us to rectify a trajectory, explore new orientations, experiment another way of life."
Carl Gustav Jung.

As soon as a thought about the past crosses your mind, repeat the mantra 'IN PRESENCE' or 'NOW'.
Thus, your attention will turn to the present, on what is happening around you and not on worn out and stale projections of the past.
You can only act in the present.
It's in the instant that you create your life.
It's within each moment that you have the means of transforming it either into a Homo Deus evolution or into a path that is disconnected from your true nature.

Release of your need to recall the past.
Release of your need to keep photos, videos,
writings of your past.
Release of your need to think that
the past influences your present or future.
End of your struggles to heal,
to remain fit and to live at all costs.
YOU ARE EVERYTHING.

STEP 10

You no longer need to worry about the future

You don't have to have any more anguish over the future because you no longer have a past. Now it is only someone having already endured hardship and trauma who can fear the future. When you have a clean slate without history or memory, everything is possible and you have faith in whatever arises.

Nothing nor nobody can predict the future. It's therefore useless trying to discover it first.
Have confidence in yourself knowing that you will do your best possible in the situation that occurs.
To face the future in the best manner, you just need this total trust in yourself, in your ability to adapt and in life itself.

The future is unpredictable since it is, as all else in this universe, in perpetual change!
You have no advantage holding a pessimistic view on it. It would depress you, push you to procrastinate and would wear out your precious energy.
You have no more advantage imagining it as positive. It wouldn't change anything to what can happen sooner or later.
And mostly, imagining the future disconnects you from the present moment. And it's only in this moment that you can create/change your life!

When an idea comes to your mind, if it's possible to enact it right away, then do it: it's perfect and you received it at the ideal time.

Furthermore, if thus accomplished, it won't clutter your mind any longer. This thought will be evacuated and allow a new idea to pop up!

On the other hand, if you get an idea for an ulterior moment, other than the one you're in, write it down on paper and keep it in a place well in view. Then let go of the thought. It's of no use to you for the time being!

Transcribing your idea is the only thing to do when you get an insight about something in the future. Once it's down, release it from your mind, this will allow new ideas to come enrich your life!

It's pointless to clog your mind with negative, redundant or denigrating thoughts.

Your mind and your life will get on better if you don't pursue these inner monologs. Let them pass without any attempt to grab hold or develop them.

If you fear a disastrous future for the planet and its inhabitants, well then act now by creating each minute into an ideal PRESENT.

In concrete terms, change your consumer habits by adding conscience and good sense: Live up each day to the values, which you would like to see, implanted in this world.

You would like for peace to reign between human beings?

Be at peace. Don't judge anyone. Love your toxic mother-in-law, your noisy neighbor, your revolting colleague, your too demanding boss, your exhausting children, this abominable criminal, this myth maniac president…

You wish there was abundance for everyone?
Don't search for the lowest price. Because to arrive at such a price, bosses have to exploit their workers and use toxic and poor quality products. And this at thousands of miles from your home in order to reduce the margin of manufacturing costs while increasing their own profits and those of their stock holders.
Remember that for the time being, money rules this world. And the stock exchange is where the money is.
Therefore if you want a fair and equitable distribution of goods, you must buy local and sustainable products and foods. Thus you will allow people in your own country to work in decent conditions. In addition, you will help to reduce pollution and the massive energy use of transport. And you shall stop financing the exploitation of populations from third world countries.
In short, avoid as you can supermarkets, multinational corporations, banks, savings accounts, insurances and stock investments.

Are you afraid of overpopulation? We are too many on earth?
Wrong. The planet has an abundance of drinking water, food and space to accommodate its inhabitants however many there may be. The only reason for this 'illusion' of scarcity and overpopulation is the unfair distribution of wealth…

We are not too many, there are only 1% of humans in surplus actually and these 1% are the bankers and billionaires which have appropriated all the wealth for their personal benefit!

Consider that 1% of the population owns more than the other 99% combined. Thus, sixty-two people are richer than four billion individuals. And you can be sure that they aren't the ones who will alter things for a more equitable share.

If all the people lived in the country and in nature rather than piling up in polluted cities, if each person grew fruits and vegetables in his/her own village and surrounding land, if each person would save the pits and seeds of the food he/she eats and sow them while for example going for a walk (or even just throw them on the side of dirt roads), if people built houses using natural materials in accordance with the available elements found near the site, if we would re-tie social relations with neighbors and use mutual aid in a brotherly fashion, if we would concentrate on local, hand-made, organic productions and permaculture, we could then see how generous this Mother earth really is!

Let's cease to constantly criticize our government and its bleeping management of the nation. Let's put away the very idea of a 'nation', of borders and division. Let's retrieve our personal power and bear in mind that it's the working class people that create wealth!

The bosses just give out orders, collect and take the fruit of their employees' labor. Let's stop calling on them to manage our own work.

You find that the quality of the cultural level is dropping and becoming poorer each day?
By praising lower instincts, unbridled sexuality, rejection of others, racism, competition, stupidity, malignancy, and regarding the body as an object to be marketed?

Forget the TV and the radio. Watch instead Internet channels which match your aspirations, your values, your aesthetic and intellectual thirsts.

Give credit to atypical and authentic films by watching them. Support writers through the purchase or rental of their books. Visit museums, which exhibit works that turn you on. Listen to harmonious and joyful music. Give art lessons, or music, dance, sport, circus, or singing classes to your children and friends.

In brief, support culture in areas which you would like to see remain.

You don't trust modern medicine anymore because it has brought about too much medical inadvertence, incorrect diagnoses, medicine on the market that is hazardous to your health, and antibiotics prescribed at any occasion?

Avoid as much as possible conventional medicine and pharmaceutical remedies. Use natural products, essential oils, tinctures of plants, homeopathy…

Consult alternative medicine practitioners such as homeopaths, osteopaths, kinesiologists, ancient Chinese medicine, acupuncture, bioenergetics and naturopaths.

You hate how banks manage their money? Manufacture and sale of weapons, stupendous interest rates for the wealthier, tax optimization and tax havens, chronic indebtedness of the poor due to enormous bank charges and consumer credit, a rising public debt established to keep an upper hand over state affairs…
You hate the fact that banks control governments and therefore the nations?

Stop entrusting them with your savings. Find other ways to safe-keep your money. It's sure that you won't miss the interests because soon we'll even have to pay the banks for them to keep our money!

You find it preposterous how your government administers your country? Yet more and more freedom-oppressive laws and precariousness for workers, farmers, the unemployed, the retired. And less and less budget for schools, hospitals, public transport, culture, prisons, social aids…
Too much expenditure on the army and police. The persistence with which the government ignores the demands and opinions of the people. The fact that our leaders in France are selling lucrative public property to private enterprises generating enormous profit such as highways, the SNCF (French railway system), the Poste, EDF (electricity of France), the French gaming society (La Francaise des Jeux) and soon the airport of Paris…

So, you can quit your salaried job, avoid toll highways, earn less to reduce income tax to a minimum, create your own job by listening to your passions and ideas, change your electricity provider, stop voting, learn by yourself, let go of the obligation of having to obtain diplomas or certificates…

But don't make these changes thinking that you're a savior or a hero.
No. You're perfect just as you are, you don't need to assume any role to legitimize your presence on earth.
Simply, act with a sense of equity towards each and every one because you know that we are ONE.
Thus, YOU treat YOURSELF with love, respect and consciousness.

Here again, murmur the mantra 'IN PRESENCE' or 'NOW' to bring your conscience back to what's here and now.
Focus your attention on the information that your senses are receiving now.
Feel the contact of your clothes on your skin, the sensations of the sun on your face, of the wind blowing on your hair, your tongue pushing on your palate, your feet laying on the tiles, of your hand holding a glass of water, your eyes observing the sky, of your ears hearing the humming sound of the truck afar on a construction site, of the taste of the apple you've just chewed…
Your five senses are open windows to the present moment! It's pointless trying to figure out what is happening other than in this 'sensory reality'.
Your anger, fear or sadness can be quickly appeased as soon as you draw your attention on your physical sensations rather than on anxious thoughts.

Emotions are information. They are not to be evaluated as 'positive' or 'negative'.
They are neither unpleasant nor pleasant; they just pass through you at a certain time. They deliver you a message informing you on what behavior to adopt at the moment you receive them (to leave or to stay, to speak or not to speak, to check if the emotion is accepted or not…)
They also inform you on your perceptions, on your fears.
Love yourself and accept yourself as you are now.
Don't fight and try to elude confrontation with pain or fear. Look at it face to face. Love it. Love yourself.

**Release of your need to organize, manage, prepare, predict, ensure, assume or fear the future.
Release of heavy thoughts cluttering your mind.
Learn to see through them, by making them transparent and unsubstantial.
YOU ARE EVERYTHING.**

STEP 11

Become a vegan.

You're now ready to leave aside all industrial and unnatural foods.
Leave the eggs to chickens, the milk to calves and lambs.
Leave the honey to bees.

Bite into a fresh fruit; **eat vegetables that are raw or cooked and lightly spiced or marinated with herbs in olive oil.**
Vegetable oil that is first cold pressed is excellent to the health, contrarily to what the media say about it…while sugar is to be avoided as much as possible.

You no longer need to appease your cravings, your frustrations, and your fear with food.
You no longer need to 'fill' yourself up with food.
You don't need anything nor anybody because you are ALL.
Understand that you were eating mostly to quiet down your anguish, to 'bite' your pain and swallow your anger.
Do yourself the dishes and desserts you feel like eating. Prepare them conscientiously.
Don't allow your thoughts to wander away while you're cooking.
When you're peeling a carrot, feel this action, live it intensely. Thank the carrot!
When you're stirring a sauce, observe the sensations and smells enveloping you. Thank the ingredients!

When you're kneading a loaf of bread, become fully aware of the dough's resistance, of its consistency, of the effort your arm has to make. Thank the bread!
Love and thank EVERYTHING.

Men have been eating meat and dairy products since the earliest times…
So it has been. But the path which humanity is treading on now will lead him beyond those archaic practices.
Until you reach the divine version of yourself that is light years away from your prehistoric ancestors.
Now, the transformation is done by also modifying your diet to be more light and digestible. So that it takes up less space in your daily life.

Find out on the subject by following your intuition. You must understand that you are not only this body of flesh moving about in a three dimensional world. No, you are much more than that…

You have many other bodies visible and invisible to the naked eye, namely:
The physical body, the etheric body, the emotional body, the mental body, the causal body and the christ-like (or Buddha-like) body. It's the latter one which you're incarnating each day a bit more. And only this one is timeless, changeless, and immortal.
When the physical, emotional and mental bodies (the three densest bodies) are perfectly aligned, that is to say in agreement and tuned together, then your Homo Deus body will be able to manifest itself in matter.

As man possesses several visible and invisible bodies, so do animals, plants and even minerals.

Most animals don't have a mental body (this body enables the ego and the conscience of its individuality to exist).

Whereas plants and minerals have neither a mental nor an emotional body (this body contains the whole range of our feelings).

Nonetheless, "a body which develops, evolves and reproduces itself is alive, and all life springs from a conscience," explains Alyna Rouelle, author of the book "Nutrition and freedom".

This truth applies to humans, animals, insects, plants, microscopic cells, etc.

So, love the apple you're about to chew, love the pasta in your plate, love the basil garnished tomato.

And give thanks, out loud or silently, for each meal and parcel of food, before tasting it.

In the old days, this ritual was called 'Blessings' or 'Grace'. Our forefathers were right. Let's discover anew the sacred character of things because we have denatured, desacralized what is around us each day.

Know that you are a magnificent energy beam, a pure and vibrant light that came on this planet in order to transcend the illusion of being a poor creature, victim of elements exterior to itself.

In truth, there is nothing outside of you since you are EVERYTHING.

You're the inside AND the outside. You are the creator AND the creature.

**Release of your need to eat food
that is rich and heavy to digest.
Release of your need to eat food
made up of sensitive and living beings.
YOU ARE EVERYTHING.**

STEP 12

Drink some water, more water and still more water.

If there is a point that is common to all elements in this universe, it's that they are all made up of at least one molecule of water.

As incredible as it may seem, the presence of water has been detected on the sun!
It only persists a few seconds but is continuously reformed elsewhere on the solar disc.

The body of a man is made up of 65% of water. That of a three-day old embryo is 95% water! We are like condensed water.
Water symbolizes life.

Our society would like to have us think that drinking water is commonplace, mundane, even boring.
The media promote drinks that are sweet, sparkling, fizzy, milky and alcoholic…none of them however reaches the perfection of a single drop of water.
Our body yearns to be quenched by clear water.

It is certainly not a coincidence that this element holds a central place in many religions!
Water washes away sins, water purifies the body and the mind, water is used for ablutions, water is blessed and water is used for baptism. In short, water is sacred.

The rain, the sea, rivers and lakes are honored, thanked, celebrated.
Water cleans you from the inside. Like a wave, water diffuses a healthy flow throughout your organism.

When you feel a great surge of anger rising, drink a cup of water then observe how harmony returns to you.
When you're tired, drink some water.
When you're depressed, drink some water.
When you're anguished about the future, drink water and repeat the mantra *'In Presence'*. Very soon your mental, emotional and physical bodies will regain quietness.
Water brings your attention to the present moment.
The water hydrating you and the air you breathe will recall your attention to the fact that there is only one reality. The one you're living NOW.

Love the perfection of water. Bless it and thank it each day.
Water flows through you, water lives in you, water crosses through you from top to bottom. Water is you. Water is Everything.

Lay your hands above the water you're about to drink and energize it with your 'power' of intent.
Confer to it a quality that would be useful to you at this instant.
For example, 'Calmness' or 'Abundance'.
Water integrates the information you give to it.
This unknown process holds many secrets and numerous mysteries, which go beyond our imagination!

Along the way of the forty steps leading to your Homo Deus state, you shall go beyond all paths, above all which is known, beyond this limited universe of matter.
You shall become conscious that you are ALL! Your egotistical character shall merge with whom you really are.
And water is a bridge to take you there softly.
Drink each sip in conscience. Feel the cascade of freshness filling your body.

When your throat/mouth seems dry, it's the signal that your body sends you to alert you that it needs to be hydrated.
So, don't have it wait: drink water.

Find out about the work of Masaru Emoto.
Masaru did experiments proving that thoughts (positive, negative or neutral) have a direct influence on water.

Water is a marvelous substance of which too many people still ignore all the capacities.
You can 'inform' water in your glass to 'awaken' its ability to heal this, or to comfort that or to reinforce such or such organ.
Water carries 'memory'.

Remember also that water is you, since you are everything...
Beyond the veil of illusion, become aware that you are part of ALL because only the ALL or the ONE exists.

**Release and purification of your spirit, your mind, your emotions and your body by the cleansing and regenerating power of water.
YOU ARE EVERYTHING.**

STEP 13

Live and act in the PRESENT!

Only the present moment counts.
Forget the past, the past is already past.
Don't think about the future, the future is yet to come.
Live intensely in the present.

As soon as a thought crosses your mind, observe it calmly and ask yourself the following question:
'Does this thought concern me now?'
If yes, do what it suggests.
If no, let it go because it's of no use now.

For example, you have a sudden urge to call your brother.
The question to ask yourself:
'Can I do this here and now?'

-If yes, do it. Don't wonder whether it's the right day or not, or if you wouldn't prefer to read on the couch or watch the end of the film…do now what your idea suggests.
And thus, free your mind of that thought which, if not heeded to, shall keep returning until it is.

-If not, it's impossible to call him now (because it's midnight or you are driving at this moment…), so let go of the idea. It doesn't concern the present moment; it's not applicable now.
Don't let it hamper you.

Let it go to unburden your train of thoughts. This will allow a new idea to pop up. And this one shall perhaps be more apt, more perfect in the situation you're living now.

Be 'in presence' to what you're experiencing.
Focus your attention to what you're doing; you're in the moment.
This instant is your only reality. Live it up to the brim.
On the other hand, detach yourself from the notion of the present with respect to temporality.
You're not living in a 'present' with respect to a past or a future. No. If it were so this 'present' would just be point on a temporal line with a before and an after. It would thus be limiting.
But you are ALL! You're an incarnated aspect of the Universal Conscience without beginning nor end. You're ALWAYS in this eternal present even if you're not conscious of it.

In presence, you see at last with the eyes of the heart: on every spot where you fix your gaze Love appears.
Whether it be a cute kitten or a ferocious wolf, a butterfly or a venomous scorpion, they are all as important and perfect in your eyes.
Whether it be the worst criminal man has ever known or Mother Teresa, you look at them with love and you greet their presence on earth.
Because you know deep inside that each of them has a part to play in this comedy called life. And they have forgotten that they were issued from the Great All.
That they represent parts of darkness that you refuse to see in yourself.

That they are also there to force you to step out of your comfort zone, to push you to make the great dive towards your divinity.
THANK them. Love them as you love yourself, with your faults and imperfections.

Be fully conscious of your body, of your feelings each instant.
Accept the present moment, it is continually manifesting itself. Savor this almost palpable instant. Receive the idea, which crosses your mind, and materialize it right away when possible. If not let it pass without any further thought.

'IN PRESENCE' is the key to inner happiness.
Laughter and song are two other keys. They allow you, in all situations, to go beyond your fears and to dissipate any anxious mood weighing heavily on you.

The universe is ruled by a host of physical laws such as gravity, for example.
Even so, there is a law not so well known called the law of Attraction, which is crucial. In fact, it could well be in an extension to the law of gravity.
The book "The Secret" by Rhonda Byrne describes this law in detail in order to better comprehend the subtle mechanisms of life.

Thanks to the law of Attraction, nothing happens by chance. Everything is always a manifested return of something you've thought, said or did.

This is how your beliefs define and shape your life!
It is therefore of the utmost importance to know this law in order to adjust your behaviors and attitudes. This shall bring real change in your everyday life.

Release from your need to be attached to a past or a future.
Extreme simplification of your system of reference while remaining constantly aware of the present moment.
YOU ARE EVERYTHING.

STEP 14

Free-will is an illusion.

First of all, do you believe to be the captain in charge of your life? Do you believe to be the master of your choices? Nothing is less certain…
Observe your speech and your actions: they are the logical extension of your thoughts.
Now your thoughts arise spontaneously!
A continual flow of thoughts appears in your mind without your being able to detect their origin.
You are incapable to stop or prevent them from invading your head. At the most, through concentration, you can begin a new subject of reflection…
Nonetheless, this uninterrupted monolog will end up taking you back in its wake without your ability to control it.
Yes, you can level your thoughts once they are already there. Thus, you can hang on to those you like and let go of those you don't.
Besides a few exceptions, you don't decide what your next thoughts will be!
Now 'your' thoughts are at the origin of your actions, of your choices and of your 'personality'.
The fact that you believe to be the only one to direct your life is therefore an illusion. That's right, another one!

Secondly, free-will is a delusion because you're constantly being manipulated without even knowing it…

Society, the media, culture, family and school all influence your choices. So you're not really the master of your decisions.
If you get married, is it because married life or the ceremony gives you a thrill or is it because your parents are married, your friends are married, characters in films are also married and everything in modern or ancient culture urges you to?
You wouldn't act the same if you were from Africa or China. However, you would be the same person with the same ego.
So then, what defines your personality, your character?
Do you eat meat because your body and conscience have really decided so? Or is it your education, your peers, commerce, advertising, books and media, which push you to do it?
Before the 'fashion' of vegetarianism, perhaps you had never asked yourself the question. This act seemed obvious to you. But was it for all that your own decision?

What if, as of today, you would question EVERYTHING about your life?
Working, putting your money in the bank, having a credit card, being monogamous, wearing shoes, getting dressed, when and what you eat…
You could examine each detail of your way of life through the lens of your attentive conscience.
Scrutinize minutely each area of your daily life and find what really suits you.
At that point at last, you can begin to feel the beginning of what is free-will.

Observe your thoughts. Can you trace the source from which they emanate? How does this continuous train of thought form itself? Where does it come from?
Are you at the origin of the thoughts crossing your mind? No. They come from nowhere and are going nowhere.
You give them your interest only while they are passing…
You can also place your attention on the 'void', which briefly passes between two thoughts. Rather than focusing on the thoughts themselves.

What if you just let go of this uninterrupted stream?
What if this stream of thought didn't really belong to you, but that you 'pick it up' like a radio receiver picks up one wavelength rather than another?
Observe your thoughts from a distance. Don't grab hold of them. Leave them for those who wish to assimilate them and call them their own. But you can step away from this illusion.
You evolve between all these 'trains of thoughts', these waves running alongside of you. They do not concern you anymore. You are no longer a 'radio receiver'. You are.

**Release of your guilt of all the comings
and goings already done in your life,
because you become conscious that
everything is perfect, everything has a purpose,
even if the reason goes beyond your understanding.
You can place your life in the 'hands'
of Absolute Consciousness, of Love, because that's
where your stream of thoughts comes from!
YOU ARE EVERYTHING.**

STEP 15

'Unity' or 'Duality'.

This step shall lead you to integrate **the difference between 'Unity' and 'Duality'.**
It's the basis of Awakening.

You live in a world which appears dual: for each thing, there exists its opposite.
Black/White, Small/Big, Good/Bad, Young/Old, Yin/Yang, Above/Below, Me/Others, Woman/Man…
Now the Homo Deus shall be manifest when you are fully conscious of being ONE.
For this, you will need to assimilate in your cells that this dual world is a theater play in which you experiment what you are not: duality. Since you are EVERYTHING.
It's as if a billion individual hairs waged war against each other although being part of the same hair, of the same body!
Everything that exists is issued from the one and same origin/energy. The latter is discovering itself through a myriad of facets.

This world of illusion can be symbolized by a theater in which actors, as soon as they go up on stage, play, deliver, recite, and interpret their lines and characters.
Thus, one is the father of the other. Another loves one and hates another. A third is the bad guy who kills the good guy. Then they weep for the dead and the killer regrets already his act, or not.

But the story isn't the real issue which is after that the red curtain goes down at the end of the play, when the actors return to salute their public while holding hands, feeling alive, knit together and happy to have felt this abundance of emotions, of love, of fear and sorrow.
They are filled by the rich experience they have lived in their flesh.
Meanwhile, the public warmly thank the actors who managed so well to make them understand the nature of their feelings, the greatness of their hopes, and the misery of their wrath!
Side by side, the comedians of the company are reunited in brotherly love.

Such is life: a tragic comedy played by actors (us) who believe in it wholeheartedly. Thus, we mix ourselves up with the role that is opposite to our true nature.
And when one play is completed, another one is on its way…
Through an endless cycle, actors again play new parts, new lives. And thus since the dawn of humanity.

How to be released from this infernal cycle?
How to end with this play going from bad to worse?
By remembering and integrating the fact that all the actors are one and the same identity. A unique, perfect and changeless energy.
As soon as the 'actors' cease to interpret their role, the play stops automatically and the red curtain drops!
Truly, there are neither spectator, nor actor nor theater. Only a powerful vibration of love creating the necessary illusions to become conscious of itself.

Through this collective amnesia, which is the rule on our planet, we have become totally convinced to be the characters we play.
Up until now, you've regularly changed roles while playing in identical scenarios, like a film on automatic replay.
Since eons, you haven't managed to dissociate yourself from the restrained character who is a thousand leagues from who you really are.
Because you ARE. That's ALL.
You are ALL.

Each time that you see someone, say to yourself 'I am him/her. He/she is me.' Or 'I love him/her. I love myself.'
Each time you eat something, become aware that you are eating 'yourself' and nourishing 'yourself'.
Quit being fooled by the illusion of duality.

A fact which has changed my life is the existence of a type of toxic personality: the Narcissistic Pervert (NP).
Apparently, NP's are much more common than we think. And because they are undetectable, or even deemed above reproach by their entourage (above and foremost by the victim), no one is aware of their dangerousness.
On the other hand, you may more easily spot their victims because the latter are either under pressure, ready to strike or get angry with anyone, or they have turned amorphous, subdued or are continually exhausted.
Thus, become conscious that there exists a sort of individual who thinks only by and for him/herself at the expense of others. Through manipulation, humiliation and

lies, he/she keeps a prey (or several) under his/her control for years if not for life.
Each NP makes its victim depressive and suicidal, progressively forcing it to severe ties with relatives in order to keep the upper hand.

Once you have learned to recognize the sometimes disproportionate reactions and the methods of submitting others of these toxic individuals, it will be easier to flee from them. Don't ever try to change them, they have neither the desire nor the ability to. Following an early trauma, they have definitely cut themselves off from their source of love and empathy.
In the present, they are like parasites sucking the joy of living out of their prey.
Perhaps you have an NP parent, an NP brother, NP partner, NP boss or even an NP child. It is crucial that you be able to discern the presence of these NP's because it will help you to recover your personal power and vitality.
It's a waste to devote your time or attention to them because they will NEVER have enough. Moreover, in the process they'll empty you of your motivation and self-esteem.

It is necessary to see them as they really are in order to let them manage their own life without allowing them to spoil yours.
For example, if your father is an NP, you can still visit him but you won't share with him your innermost feelings and you won't be affected anymore by his acrid remarks about you nor by his ceaseless complaints. You will have understood that the problem lies in him, not in yourself.

Don't try to change him any longer. You'll love him such as he is while keeping a safe distance.
Above all, you'll protect yourself from his manipulative attempts and emotional blackmail.

Humanity is becoming increasingly aware of these so-called humans manipulating and exhausting them. Thanks to this knowledge, people will be able with greater facility to pinpoint NP's and avoid them.
Deprived of their needed prey in order to survive each day, the era of narcissistic perverts is on the verge of ending.
Since untold ages, these energy parasites have done all to hide from us our sacred essence and the knowledge of who we really are.
Freed at last from its noxious enslavement, tomorrow's humanity will become the most beautiful version of itself. That is to say, the Homo Deus.

**Release yourself from your fear of the other.
Release yourself from fear of life's difficulties,
of injustice and victimization, while remembering
that you are also the other and that you are life.
YOU ARE EVERYTHING.**

STEP 16

Let go of your expectations, your desires, your hopes.

Your expectations always give you the impression of being incomplete.
Your hopes make you believe that later, it will be better.
But no, everything is already here now. Everything that you need is here!

You're in the midst of an ever moving dance, why do you try to fix on an element in this total impermanence?
Your hopes generate suffering. Either because you expect something, or you're afraid to lose what you're so happy to possess.
Your acts won't be the same if you do them only for pleasure, without purpose, without trying to attain some goal.
For example, if you write a book with the hope of being published by a prestigious editor and to make it a bestseller, you won't write with the same liberty than if you're only guided by your strong desire to tell an inspiring story. The end result won't at all be the same!

Be without expectation and thus without judgment with respect to yourself or to your work.
Listen to your aspirations without expecting any reward or wanting to obtain attention, love, recognition or notoriety.
Recognize your real drives. Those spontaneous drives which push you to create, to materialize an action, a

project, to have it pass from the state of idea to that of accomplishment.
Detect within yourself impulses that are free and serene, to let them grow and become reality.
Don't be afraid to fail. The path you follow is what's important, not whether or not you arrive at destination.
Forget about negative judgments, criticisms and the denigration you keep inflicting upon yourself without even realizing it…
Your thoughts are continually putting you down, comparing and depreciating you with respect to others.
Why do you give so much credit to this rebarbative thinking?

Act according to your conscience.
Don't take into account what your ego keeps harping on about.
Flee from discourse claiming you have to work to live, that work is pleasant to no one and that it's advisable to do like others.
Because these people speak out of their own fears, their own beliefs. But they aren't on the same path of personal development as you are.
The majority of people have no idea of what they really are.
They are blinded by the 'matrix' and this world of illusion. They are still asleep…
They aren't on the same wavelength as you.
They're at their own level on the way of their inner evolution. You don't need to explain your vision to them but they don't need to impose theirs on you.

To each his/her own rhythm. To each his/her own truth. To each his/her own blocks and limited beliefs.
Now that you're working to become a Homo Deus, you have no need to adhere to old retrograde values and narrow thinking.
YOU ARE, therefore you are LIMITLESS!

What a relief when you let go of your expectations! At last you can be happy 'now'!
You've succeeded in being joyful without any reason outside of yourself! Wow!
What freedom!
Imagine yourself, here and now, to be in the skin of the ideal person, of the ideal human.
Visualize yourself as having EVERYTHING you need, with nothing missing.
Feel the perfection which encompasses your being.
Thus, it's already accomplished. Everything is done.
Be yourself. BE!
This is how you can live each day.
Be that person who is in total harmony with him/herself and the world at large.
Be that one who accepts his/herself as he/she is and loves his/herself unconditionally.

Detect, hear and follow your ideas, your deep yearnings.
Materialize them.

Observe your fear of not succeeding. Accept this fear. Give love to it. Transcend it.
And do anyway what your heart is telling you to do.

Allow no more for rigid and anguished thought patterns to direct your life. They have no authority to validate or refute the idea which you're craving to realize. So what if the project is 'profitable' or 'feasible' or not?
Do it if such is your aspiration. Listen to that 'inner fire'; it will be your best guide.
While you are realizing your projects, keep on following your ideas, they will guide you in a wonderful way.
There isn't any failure, only pleasant or unpleasant experiences, but always enriching and necessary.

Abandon the hope of accomplishing projects according to a well defined plan. Let yourself be surprised by life!
In fact, perhaps you won't make any money through your passion, nevertheless you'll still live abundantly enough because your livelihood will come via 'indirect' ways:
an inheritance, a spouse, a sponsor, a grant, a competitive examination, rent from a property, an allowance or a housing voucher, savings,…
Accept the state of what is and then thank yourself for being able to experiment through it detachment and humility.

Abundance can also become manifest with a low income but with even less spending. On the other hand, some people make a fortune but suffer lack or are indebted because they spend way above their means…

Your ideas will even help you to find housing, a vehicle, furniture, clothes and food for free or cheap! Thanks to the unsold, to fast sales, second-hands, clearance sales, thrift shops, to carpooling, and co-rentals, the gathering of fruit in nature, to the self-administered or local exchange currencies, to donations, house-sittings, abandoned objects on the sidewalk…

When you have faith in it, the universe shows much inventiveness in providing that which you need. It seems to love using unsuspected byways and not the conventional schemes.

Everything is possible as soon as you let your heart speak!

**Release yourself of any expectation of an answer
whether it be through a mail, or a candidacy,
a state exam, or from a real estate agent, a banker…
Release yourself from having
to have someone else validate what you do,
appreciate you or give affection to you.
Everything is already there.
Everything is perfect as it is.
YOU ARE EVERYTHING.**

STEP 17

Let go of all your fears.

Welcome your fears in order to get rid of them definitely and go forward.
Fear of abandonment, fear of rejection, fear of being different, fear of humiliation, fear of not being loved, fear of being loved, fear of pain, fear of disease, fear of fear, fear of death…
Let go of your fears then see how light it feels!

Fear gnaws at you from inside. It eats you away, exhausts you and drains you.
You've got no hold on either life or events. On the other hand, you can work on accepting things that happen without judging them.
Neither good, nor bad. Everything is perfect. Everything is an experience to live in this temporary physical body.
You're on earth to experiment what in fact your pure essence is not: your real nature has neither fear nor hate. You are only Love.

For each word, each thought, each choice, each action, **always choose Love and not fear**.
95% of your fears will never happen! They are imaginary and irrational.
Nevertheless they literally paralyze you day after day…
Try to reckon the number of hours in your life that you've spent worrying for absolutely nothing!

And the 5% of fear based on actual danger, which you managed to avoid most of the time because you saw it coming. Or else it was unavoidable and your fear could not change it.

To get rid of a fear, there is a solution through a threefold process:

1- You face up to this fear.
Stop lying to yourself on the existence of this phobia, of this paralyzing fear.
Sincerely acknowledge that you're afraid of whatever it may be.

2- You love it as it is and you love yourself as you are.
Accept this fear. You honor its existence knowing that everything is perfect and that, in spite of being ignorant of its causes, this fear has a part to play in your evolution.
You accept that this fear dwells in you and you cease to fight against it, to reject it.
Treat it as information, like a message sent to your body and soul.
If you receive a letter, which seems unpleasant to you, are you going to spit on its envelope, burn it, tear it up, ignore it, insult it? No. The unpleasant feeling is legitimate. You see it, accept it, love it, you allow it to deliver its message to you, you accept this message and go on to the last step to transmute the fear.

3- You act
You live through it peacefully and calmly. It isn't going to dictate what your manners and choices are to be any longer.
You're confident deep within. You know that behind the majority of your unfounded fears lies a hidden evolutionary step towards your total freedom!
You start to act and to do what your fear prevented you from doing.
If that seems like too much at once, you can also go at it progressively, one step at a time. But to vanquish this fear you'll eventually need to do that action which you prevented yourself from doing.
You'll soon understand that most of the time, your fears were hiding away from you some marvelous gifts of life!

Example: Are you phobic to drive a car?
1- Look at reality square in the face: you are a victim of this phobia which is preventing you to be free and to drive off when and where you want.
2- Love this fear, don't suppress it anymore. Accept it as a part of you for the time being. Listen to it when it enters your thoughts.
Talk to it: *"Yes, dear fear, I understand you. You are right, driving is a big responsibility. I love you. Thanks for cautioning me not to take driving lightly."*
3- Sign up for a course at a driving school. Ask a friend/parent to accompany you on a few trips to make sure you're not doing any mistakes, to reassure until you feel ready to drive alone. Stay connected to your desire to

sit behind the wheel rather than having someone else to drive you around.

Each day, work gently on transcending your fear.

Thus, you progress, step after step, on the way of acceptance of your fears and of extending your limits, while respecting your own rhythm, without expectations, without judgment or self-denial.

Each time you become afraid, don't avoid this uncomfortable feeling. Look at it in the eye!

Try to discover the origin of your fear and accept this emotion, which isn't your enemy but a faithful friend showing you the point to work on in order to evolve.

Find the cause generating this fear then act.

Do what your fear is blocking you to do, except if this action puts you in real danger (for example, leaning too much over the top of a bridge is really dangerous. On the other hand, asking for a raise to your boss isn't).

Keep in mind that *'fear is a liar'* and that *'fear is a poor counselor.'*

Analyze the actions you've made or haven't made because of fear. This will highlight the counterproductive counsel induced by your fear, because it ignores the projects of the great ALL.

Your 'mental body' breathes fear into your 'emotional body'. Now the knowledge of your mental body is limited because founded only on lived out experience.

Listen to your intuition, that little voice, trusting, discreet and always filled with Love. Because its messages come

from your soul which, unlike your mental body, is connected to the omniscient Conscience.
Your soul knows ALL about EVERYTHING. Its counsel is so much more precious, pertinent and perfect!

If you obey your fear, you create a world made in its image: stressful, frightening, limited and enslaving.
If you obey the counsel of Love, you set a world of joy, autonomy and abundance.
From now on, try loving your fear and going beyond it: go tell this person that you love him/her, sing at a karaoke if you haven't dared to before, spend a weekend all by yourself, send your manuscript to an editor, sign up at a flamenco or piano course, invite your father with whom you're out of sorts, tell your employer that he doesn't have the right to treat you disrespectfully…
Did these example give echo to any of your fears? Nevertheless, they don't represent any danger to your life, quite on the opposite.

The innate automatic reflexes, which our body is conditioned to use as soon as fear manifests itself, are the following:
Escape, paralysis or attack.

These three attitudes are in our genes since the dawn of ages.
But our evolution as a Homo Sapiens is tending towards becoming a Homo Deus, thus having no more use of this old program of primitive survival. It has become obsolete to the new generation of divine beings.

The hour of transformation has come. At last, the caterpillar is turning into a butterfly.

**Release of your fears. They'll appear in their own time. Accept them lovingly without judging. They merge and unite with you. Your fears disappear one after another. You reconnect to the state of unlimited individual now that fear no longer paralyses you.
YOU ARE EVERYTHING.**

STEP 18

Adopt a raw diet.

You eat what is essential.
You hardly ever feel hungry anymore.
Usually - with a few exceptions - when we eat, it's often to fill a void, an inner emptiness, a gnawing fear…And not for any real need of the body.
If you would only eat when your stomach cries out to you starving, you would only ingest a third, at the most, of what you do each day.
Now that you're detaching yourself from your ego, you no longer have any lack to replete nor fear to choke. You may leave your digestive system alone and feed it only when a vital need is really felt.

No more sweet pastries, useless desserts and copious meals.
No more alcoholic aperitifs, salted crackers and other snacks used to calm down your stress.
Detect the signals that your body sends you for lack of water or food.
Eat only to nourish yourself.
If you still have doubts, see what sort of food you feel like having…
If it's food that is simple (raw) and natural, then hunger is your guide. Otherwise, your appetite is a lure to appease inner tension.

A cooking process above 104 degrees F partly destroys vitamins and other nutrients found in fruits and vegetables, which therefore become less digestible to your organism.

Eating natural and healthy ingredients are a token that you're not just eating to ease strong emotions.
Because if you are still prey to irresistible snacks, it means that your thoughts and emotions are still in charge of your life. The ups and downs of your emotional body still dictate your behavior.
Now remember that you are ALL. You're not just this human. You are the incarnated Universal Conscience, Love experimenting with itself.
You are all of the protagonists in this adventure so you may love and respect them all, starting with yourself.
Let go of those self-indulgent munchies. You don't need anything.
Follow the path of light on which you will soon have no need for nourishment since you shall be conscious of evolving within an illusion. Others are an illusion, in the same way as you.
Nothing really exists, neither this body, nor theses planets, nor theses suns. You've created them but see yourself as a creature. You created this theater called life in order to be able to enjoy it and grow in the conscience of who you are in contrast with what you are not.

For this step, listen carefully to the messages and needs of your physical body.
If you're afraid to yield by eating something in order to calm your tensions, meditate.
On the other hand, don't fight against yourself.
Accept yourself as you are. Do what you long for, allowing yourself to fail, postpone, start over, try later…
Walk slowly in nature, re-energize yourself.

Lift your face towards the light of the sun and let yourself be warmed by its nourishing rays.
Drink much water and eat food that is the most natural as possible:
        Vegetable, Alive (raw, fresh) and Varied!

Prepare your food in full conscience.
You can meditate while you do!
Meditation is possible each instant of your life, even during chores.
The moment of preparing a meal is as precious as the meal itself.
It's about celebrating the magnificence of the food which 'Mother Nature' provides in abundance.
Making a dish is a sacred ritual, which precedes another ritual of life: nourishment.
Touching, preparing, mixing the ingredients is equivalent to entering in communion with the Universal Conscience, which takes shape in this zucchini, in these grapes, in this unctuous oil…

Let go of your habit of cooking, roasting,
frying, heating, grilling, burning the food
that you want to ingest.
Simplification of your diet
and saving of time to focus on other things.
YOU ARE EVERYTHING.

STEP 19

You are complete.

The myth of passionate love, of a soul mate or twin flame is a lure.
You don't need anybody to become the best version of yourself.
You were born complete and you have all the necessary resources already built in you.

As for **sex**, how does a Homo Deus behave in this very 'human', if not to say 'animal', domain?
The more you live out your divine conscience day by day, the more will sexual attraction for one or several other people tend to disappear.
You are eternal; you don't 'need' to reproduce to propagate the 'species'. You don't belong to any species, YOU ARE.

Your ego is no longer the master directing your life. Therefore, you don't try to seduce, nor to be desired.
Your ego is no longer there wanting to 'possess' another person, a beautiful woman or a handsome man. You are whole, complete. You are EVERYTHING.
There's no more any point of appropriating yourself of another being in order to justify your seductive powers, to legitimatize your 'worth' in the eye of your entourage.
In the same manner as your appetite for food will run out, so your 'sexual appetite' will also soon diminish. It will naturally wither away.

Your body lives in total harmony, even in autarchy. It doesn't need anything nor anyone in order to be.
It nourishes itself on pure Love, this omnipresent energy of Love, vibrating in all things, creating this universe at each moment.

When you love conditionally and when you desire someone, unconsciously you're trying to fill a void inside you. This void frightens you.
The lure is to believe that you will manage to fill your inner void by 'consuming' something outside of you.
It's a false lead. Learn to look at this void, to love it and then to personally fill it up. Thus you seal forever this gaping hole. You cease to be tributary of others and of their conditions.
Let go of always having to rely on someone, even perhaps to the point of being led by toxic, negative or despicable people, to compensate for your lacks.
Only then can true Love grow. This sentiment loves to love, loves without expectations of return and without conditions.
The time is over of having to beg someone to love you! You recover the power of satisfying your aspirations, of vanquishing your fears. Finally, it allows you to really grow in conscience.

Sex is again an illusion from our 3D world.
Don't fight to 'hush' your libido. Don't force yourself to be abstinent if your body is still calling out for it.
But follow at your own pace this path towards sexual freedom.

Aim for a definite liberation from your 'sexual needs', from having to procreate, satisfy a lack, a fear or a desire.
Keep in mind that a Homo Deus is free of all physical constraint, and not submitted to anything nor anyone.
Satisfying a sexual need is constraining, time and energy consuming and egotistical. It represents another dependence on someone or something.
A neglected libido dies off.
Perhaps released manually and naturally, without pressure, guilt nor remorse, the sexual urge will tend to decrease each day a bit more until disappearing with hardly your notice.
Of course, in parallel, avoid TV and certain films which exacerbate the lower and most vile instincts.

From the moment you cease to be 'precisely' an individual, an entity separated from the rest, then you no longer feel the necessity to form a couple, celibacy doesn't frighten you anymore.
You accept solitude, being in couple or with several partners, as it presents itself, without judgment.
EVERYTHING IS GOOD. Everything is perfect.
When the personality attached to your ego and to your name disappears, you're no longer striving to find the 'love of your life', a life companion, a housemate, a 'soul mate' or a 'twin flame'.
You don't care. You no longer worry about anything. You are free.
As your fears and needs begin to disappear, so your joy - innate, permanent and without condition - can take over your being, every day and without cause. Your joy of being blossoms!

Thus, you depart from the grip of dependence to illusory needs and go on to live a state of grace without end, in an infinity of present moments.

Delivered from this physical constraint, you shall soon bathe in constant felicity.

As soon as you see a person to whom you feel physically or sexually attracted to, remind yourself that it's certainly about an egotistical desire to "possess" him/her, a self-appropriation…

Now this desire is founded on the illusion that alone, you are not complete.

Remain calm when your libido is guiding you towards a peak that demands gratification.

Meditate, focus your attention on breathing slowly and regularly, and repeat the mantra 'In Presence', if it seems appropriate to you at that moment.

Don't fight against your sexual drive. But welcome this drive, this desire.

Yes, you have this urging need now. So be it. Must you imperatively satisfy it?

Probe within yourself to find an answer to this question.

Is it so serious if you let it pass, if you ignore it? It is for you to find the answer.

Observe this desire which seems to torment you.

Be as the observer of your incarnated person. Because you are not this being.

Furthermore, sexuality is so little well known today…although it generates powerful forces, which go way beyond the level of the genital organs.
Find out about Tantra and Tao. Document yourself on the rise of the Kundalini, on orgasmic meditations, ovarian breathing and orbital meditation…

Perhaps you may first have to become more conscious of your basic sexuality, then pass through the development of your sexual power, to finally definitively transcend all your sexual needs?
To each his/her own path, to each his/her own rhythm.
Love yourself and accept yourself such as you are, no matter how long it takes to reach the end of your needs.

Release of your need to be in couple.
Release of your need to be a parent.
Release of your need to be somebody's friend.
Release of your need to be someone's colleague.
Release of your need to be someone's child…
Release of your sexual need.
YOU ARE EVERYTHING.

STEP 20

Go on a liquid diet.
Drink only water, juices and liquids
<u>with or without</u> solids in suspension.

You now abandon solid food **to nourish yourself exclusively with fruit juices**, raw vegetable juices, broths, soups, herbal teas and pure water.

This allows your vibrational level to rise.
This fluid, light, digestible and ultra-vitamin diet will increase many times over your physical energy.
Your digestion is quick, it goes to the essential.
Since your conscience is awakening to its reality, your body and its physiological needs become lighter.
Your body is purifying itself. It doesn't tolerate too well anymore any food that is rich, complex and compact.
It yearns for more harmony.
Don't force yourself to succeed nor attempt to definitely integrate this step by constraint. Go with the flow. Follow your ideas, your wishes. Don't ever do violence to yourself through an extremist approach.
Listen to your bodily needs. One day, naturally, you might have the inkling to stop such or such solid food, preferring instead to have a vegetable soup or a freshly pressed fruit juice.
Furthermore, always remain open and attentive to your needs of the moment. Today, you may go perhaps on a 100 percent liquid diet and tomorrow, allow yourself a more solid meal?

This doesn't at all mean a 'digression' or a 'defeat'. No. Follow your own evolutionary path, your own rhythm, without forcing.
Each must listen to himself/herself. Remain supple, in the joy and love of yourself, of your body and of EVERYTHING.

Maybe you'll be able to nourish yourself for a whole season on a solely aqueous diet. Then, with the coming of winter, you might be inclined again to eat fat and solid food.
Listen to yourself. Eat what your soul suggests you.
What is done under constraint lasts only for a time.
What is done in a fluid manner persists.

If your heart and body feel up to it, prepare yourself freshly pressed fruit juices, vegetable broths with seaweed (spirulina, chlorella, klamath, wakame, sea beans and nori algae), or soups, mixed or in julienne strips.
As a transition and to reassure your mental body, you can also use 'superfoods':
Herbal juice, ginger, garlic, acai berries, acerola, carob, moringa, pure cacao, maca, nopal, guarana powder, hemp seeds…
Superfoods are so rich in minerals, vitamins, antioxidants and essential amino acids that only a minimal quantity is required.

Offer yourself a juicer to transform into juice all the fresh fruits and vegetables that nature provides. These vary with the seasons.

Each day listen to your aspirations and intuition in order to consume the foods that are proper to you.
Be in peace and acceptance if you don't manage to do this step entirely.
Trust in yourself and keep on observing your needs in order to adapt little by little.

Since the beginning of this inner transformation process, you've been progressively going towards a totally light diet, towards your dietary freedom!
The final result of this process is to become pranic, that is who feeds on light (see step 39).
There's a tremendous difference between being fed with 'prana' and fasting.
Fasting is an inner cleansing which draws on your resources and reserves.
Fasting is for a limited time only, approximately one month maximum (note that this duration is quite longer than what the mainstream media say…).

On the other hand, feeding on prana is a mode of nourishment like any other.
If you've never heard of it, it doesn't mean it doesn't exist.
To be fed with prana is a reality.
There are an increasing number of people who function this way every day since many years.
Start by getting informed on the subject. There are many books that deal with it (see the bibliography section at the end of this book).

Internet is full of testimonies of pranic people (for example, Jasmuheen or Victor Truviano).

Release yourself from the habit of ingesting food that you must bite, chew, munch, crunch, crush, ruminate… You reach the essential of nutrition.
YOU ARE EVERYTHING.

STEP 21

You're on earth to evolve from inside.

You don't have anything to prove to anyone. Neither to your parents, nor to your family, nor to your friends, nor to your entourage, nor to your neighbors, nor to your children, nor to your boss, nor to your country, nor to yourself.
You are.
You don't need anything other than to be there, here and now: IN PRESENCE.
Inside of you, you are at peace.
Everything is calm and serene in you.
You don't owe anything to anyone.
You don't have to be accountable, nor give attention, nor affection, nor anything to anyone. If you do so, it's only because you really want to, not from obligation.
It will therefore be a happy and spontaneous gift from your part, not an imposed act and done unwillingly, through some kind of pressure.

In these times of 'economic crisis', salaried jobs are becoming rare.
But it's a blessing! It's pushing people to devote more time to themselves.
Work that is disconnected from personal aspirations is disappearing. So much the better, it had only brought a superficial social status, money and an illusion of usefulness in this world.

The veils are falling off. The false 'commercial value' of a being with respect to what he contributes to society shall soon be obsolete.
The time has come to work on yourself, for your own fulfillment.
Because the physical body which you inherited at birth is a tool in itself.
Learn to tell the difference between your ideas and your thoughts.
Discover how your fears dictate your behavior, how modern society incites you to become selfish, individualistic, afraid and materialistic.
All these workings are not from you but were inculcated to you since childhood by your family, school, the media, entertainment and society…

Your existence allows you to discover who you are, what you love, the diet most suitable to you and the way of life which fits you best.
In spite of what the government and your entourage wish to make you believe, it isn't necessary to work for an employer who is stressful, despising, infantilizing, even insulting, nor to be paid a miserable salary until your retirement.
No. It's a lie. This society treats you like a labor force that is insignificant, interchangeable, worthless, dehumanized, underpaid…
You are exactly the opposite!
You are unique; you deserve consideration, respect, abundance and the best each day.
You are divine, and you are on the verge of remembering it!

But how could your divinity become manifest in matter if your thoughts, your words and actions reflect submission, superficiality, lack or poverty?

Work on yourself. Appease your fears. Increase your Love for yourself, for others, for animals, for nature, for the entire Universe. Because all things are connected.
You are them and therefore they are you.

On a daily basis, choose joy. Get away from anger or fear.
Quit thinking that without a job, without a mate, without a friend or family, you are worthless.
The value of something is a notion that belongs to the capitalist and liberal world. This financial world treats everything (humans, animals, plants, minerals, this planet) as a merchandise which needs to be profitable if not it is thrown in the waste disposal (such as male chicks that are not 'useful' in becoming laying hens).
No. The lives of beings can't be limited to a financial value, nor to any usefulness.
You are here to grow in your conscience, to become the most radiant version of yourself. Thus, by progressing always further towards more love and trust, you show the example to your kind and spread ever more love and joy on Earth.
This is what is precious. This is what's vital. This is what's essential.

Regularly reserve a full day to yourself. A day in which you don't have any plans.
No entertainment: no film, no video game, no rendezvous.
A day in which you get up naturally, without an alarm. In which you stretch and listen to the minutest of your ideas. A smoothie for breakfast, for example. Read that book, stroll along the street, lie down on your garden lawn, listen to that album, write a few lines in your diary.
A day in which you become more conscious of your body by doing some auto-massage, brushing your hair…
You can meditate, do Tai-chi, Qi gong, gymnastics or yoga.
You can watch the sky, nature, the singing birds, the passersby.
A day in which you focus your attention on your breathing, in a calm place or with contemplative music in the background.
Don't do anything for profit, nothing useful, nothing important! Just be you.
Love yourself. Love the sweetness of this day and the perfume of flowers.
Inhale long whiffs of oxygen and exhale Love.

This exercise will help you become aware that YOU ARE, that you don't need to do anything to be happy.
Be like the innocent child who plays without fretting about tomorrow or the purpose of his play.
Thus, you shall discover what wishes your aspiration naturally leads you to accomplish. Perhaps these wishes will become something you would like to do on a daily basis.

You will follow your creations in this direction, without expecting any results, without mentally judging. Just to be fully engrossed in what you do. For the love of what you're doing. Without compromise.

Vincent Van Gogh, listening only to his soul and passion, made a great number of paintings during his short life.
Success remained at bay, so he lived in great poverty until his death.
He only sold one painting during his lifetime!
Notwithstanding, today, his work is exhibited in the most prestigious museums.
He is among the top reknowned artists in the history of painting.

In final analysis, Vincent is a model to be followed. Because he responded to his heart's appeal rather than financial security or the dictates of the society in his time. Without such an ironclad will, we would not have the great joy nowadays of admiring his fascinating paintings.

Whether or not one can live from his talent, what's important is deciding to dedicate one's time to it.

**Release yourself from the need to justify your presence in this society.
Release yourself from having to defend your choice of daily programs.
YOU ARE EVERYTHING.**

STEP 22

You are immortal.

You are on earth to experiment what your pure essence is not in reality:
You are not mortal.

You are immortal. Without beginning nor end. You were never born and therefore you are never dead.
But in this world of illusions, you experiment multiple lives on multiple planets, of which this life on this planet and in this life.

Louis Pauwels in "Blumroch the admirable":
"The caterpillar wondering about his future imagines himself as a super-caterpillar."
Super-caterpillar and not butterfly...
The same goes for human beings!
Our evolution is still in progress, we haven't yet arrived at the quintessence of what humanity can become. We are caterpillars and shall become butterflies.
The butterfly represents the Homo Deus with respect to the caterpillar/Homo Sapiens that we are today.
Each caterpillar possesses the genetic material to become a butterfly. Even if the caterpillar is totally unaware of it, that remains a fact.

Look up 'Near Death Experience' on the multitude of individuals from the whole world who have lived and given personal accounts of NDE. They were clinically

dead during several seconds or minutes and then returned to life. After they tell what they've seen beyond.
If you wish, document yourself on their testimonies, their tales.
Their spirit was lucid and conscious, in spite of the death of their physical body (and therefore of their brain).
Maybe you have personally lived this experience as well? You then have no more doubts about the existence of life after death. You are even definitely reassured because you were able to feel an absolute bliss in a light described as *'a thousand suns that don't burn you'* and of which the sensation is like bathing in Pure Unconditional Love!

When our soul decides to incarnate itself on this planet, it accepts the 'pact of forgetfulness'.
The Universal conscience becomes a multitude of souls individualizing themselves during an incarnation. To do this, it erases what it knows from its memory, what it has already experimented, in order to live an earthly experience and have the unheard of privilege of 're-discovering' who it is in reality during the process referred to as -among other names - *the Awakening.*

Don't be afraid of physical death any longer because you have already been through it a billion times!
Now here you are again experimenting a terrestrial life with a new material body. This means you've already made it perfectly each time and you'll make it the following times.

Be trustful. The essential doesn't change: your soul (this drop originating and included in the Great All) is changeless, timeless and eternal. You cannot die because you were never born.
This three-dimensional world of matter reflects this to you so that you may experiment Love in all of its forms and incarnate it over and over again in a world where it isn't much valued.

Sing when you're afraid. Sing when you suffer!
Singing has an unrecognized magical power, it allows an escape from anguish in which you seem blocked.
Sing out loud or in your head, but sing when you realize that your thoughts are bogged down in a negative slump.

Sing and smile! It will heighten your vibrational level.
Prepare a 'Happy play-list' with songs that are joyful, positive and light. So that you may switch it on when you feel anxious or when sadness monopolizes your mind…

**Release yourself from the need of making
your time profitable, of immortalizing such
or such important event,
Release your need of having 'to do something'
before leaving this earth, to find your path,
to accomplish your 'life's mission', to leave a trace,
a heritage, mark history…
YOU ARE EVERYTHING.**

STEP 23

You heal yourself.

If you become ill, cure yourself using methods that are ancestral, intuitive and natural, proven effective since millennia. No to modern chemistry, which entails as many if not more detrimental side-effects than beneficial ones!
With the exception of course of extreme emergency cases or if your life is in danger at that moment.

Recommended ways for self-healing are:

1- **Water that is programed and energized.**
See more explanations in step 12 about the widely unknown virtues of water.
Water has a 'memory'. It suffices to inform your water by energizing it. That is by making it swirl in a glass/bottle. You may also get hold of a *'Devajal water vitalizer'*, it's a mini-funnel creating a vortex when the water passes from one bottle to another.
To program the water, you must think or pronounce a word while the water is swirled.
You may also energize it with your hands around the recipient.
In this case, choose an information/word such as 'healing', or 'excellent health' or 'harmony'…
And finally, drink this water with conscience and gratitude. Drink it as many times as you wish. Listen to yourself.

2- Fasting.

Very distinct from being nourished with prana (See more in step 39), fasting is a natural way of cleansing the body.

Your body eliminates toxins while the digestive system is at rest since the latter must not digest nor transform anything.

A 24 hour fast will very beneficial to you in any case.

Consider that with a close upkeep and attention to his/her body, a human can fast up to 30 days before dying of hunger! A far cry from the famous: "three days without drink and seven days without food".

It is useless and dangerous to go to this limit but knowing this fact will help ease the anguish of death due to food privation.

A little reminder: to start eating normally again after a fast, it is important to go at it <u>very</u> progressively.

3- Amaroli, or 'urine-therapy' or 'Shivambu'.

Read up on this method derived from Ayurveda medicine.

This technique is astonishingly simple!

By the same token, you stop contributing to the wealth of 'Big Pharma' and pharmaceutical lobbies.

You return your trust and priority to your body while honoring its perfection and infinite resources.

You recover your power, of knowing what is good for you, of healing yourself, of being autonomous, of not entrusting your life, your money, your power and your energy to international corporations, which draw considerable profit to the detriment of their consumers' health.

If doing this practice makes sense to you, integrate it to your daily routine.

4- Letting yourself go totally to your actual state of health.
You accept your illness, not fight against it. You love it as a part of the whole, of you.
You thank it for being there, to be giving you information on your lifestyle choices that are perhaps not up-to-par with your conscience, causing your physical, mental and emotional 'bodies' to become misaligned. This eventually leads to a short or long term pathology.
Therefore, you don't expect immediate healing, nor even any at all.
You live this illness experience while being careful not to give it too much attention either. It is simply there.
You authorize your body to manage your health as it knows so well how to do.
You completely trust your physical body. It knows.
As for you, you meditate to maintain peace in your spirit and mind.

5- Laugh therapy.
See more explanations in step 5 about the countless virtues of laughter.
Laugh each day, each hour, as much as possible.
You seek the company of people that are happy, joyous and luminous.
Watch films that are comical and vibrant.
Listen to music that is up-beat, dynamic and singing.
Smile to the sun, to the rain. Laugh in the wind.
Read funny stories, jokes, inspiring novels, motivating adventures.
If your state of health allows you to:

Attend optimist and interesting conferences.
Go to harmonious or joyous concerts.
Watch a play, a performance, street theater which tends to pull you up in spirit and laughter.
As much 'feel good' activities as you want!
Each minute, remember that life is a game, a comical theater play!

A sixth approach for self-healing: **sleep**.
Rest is salutary when your body requires much energy to self-heal.
Furthermore, becoming ill is perhaps simply enough the signal sent by your body to slow it down, or even to take a short or long break!
Sometimes we prefer to blur the tiredness and burn-out messages that our body sends us, hoping that it will regulate by itself, in order to accomplish one's objectives in time.
Keep in mind that your body is a 'precious tool'. Take good care of it, as you would your house or car. Otherwise it may wear out and fall apart.

Next time you feel yourself getting ill, whether benignly or more seriously, don't rush to a doctor at the first sign of symptoms.
First, let your body act on its own.
Accept the fact of having to rest much to help your organism to heal. The notion of time of someone in convalescence is not at all the same as that of someone in good health.
Accept this difference and apply, following your intuition, the five recommendations of this step.

Homeopathy works on the principle of programed water.
Since several years, a multitude of people cure themselves through this method and heal.
Even if it argued that it's "only because they believe in it that it works" and that it's a placebo effect, it still remains valid: people really heal.
Whether out of their own volition or through homeopathy, it doesn't matter, they are healed.

In fact, this famous placebo effect is the undeniable truth that the body can self-heal.
Scientific research has demonstrated that most pharmaceutical treatments have a rate of success that is hardly above that of placebo treatments!
But they also induce a great many undesired effects as well…

**Release yourself from the need of entrusting your power and decision of treatment to another party.
Release yourself of the habit of seeking
a medical doctor before having even probed
your own feelings, body, conscience.
YOU ARE EVERYTHING.**

STEP 24

Create a world of truth.

The world of lies is living its last hours. Because you won't be feeding it anymore with your lies. Everywhere, always and in all circumstances, **choose the truth:** saying it, doing it, spreading it around each day a bit more than the day before.
We live in a world of lies and manipulation.
Good and evil, duality, the ego, separation, hierarchy…it's about lies and illusions.
Thanks to your luminous choice, transparence shall reign on earth.

Up until now, trickery and manipulation predominated in the world. Secrets, Omerta and omission played their part in keeping things opaque.
The time has come to lift the veils that conceal the truth.
Even lying by omission must be discarded from everyday life.
Speak, say what you are feeling.
Explain why you do what you do.
Don't lie anymore, neither to yourself nor to others.

You believe to be pure, honest and truthful? However, if you're sincere, you are bound to realize how much you cheat, manipulate, even gently 'for the other person's good': to convince your child to stop his/her game and come eat at table when you decide to, to keep your spouse by your side, to avoid being laughed at by your colleagues, to be loved by your parents, to be appreciated by your friends, by your entourage, by society...

You keep on playing a role that doesn't reflect your real identity by fear of rejection.

You hide your thoughts by fear of being excluded, misunderstood or despised.

So, for this new step on the path of awakening towards your divinity, you are passing into the world of truth.

Reveal your family secrets to the people concerned. Take the time to do it, find the appropriate moment to bring it up, slow up your speech to probe inside and choose the right words to illustrate your thoughts and feelings.

Dare to be yourself. Dare to reveal your sincere thoughts.

Say it in a manner that is calm, serene and well thought out, sharing your vision of the world while accepting the possibility that the person you're speaking to may disagree.

Never try to persuade others. Give your point of view if your conversation partner asks you, but without expecting anything in exchange, neither his/her approval nor his adherence.

Be ready to accept his/her reaction. Be ready to love the person who rejects you because you don't fit in his/her scheme of things.

People make their own experiences. You are not there to judge them, criticize or educate them.

They are responsible of their life just as you are of yours.

Don't hold any grudges against anyone experimenting life as he/she sees fit. It's his/her experience and in so doing,

offers you the possibility of learning how to let go of your wish of wanting to help others, of knowing better than they, of understanding more, of being right.
Remember that you are beyond the presently incarnated being...
You are not only an individual made of bone and flesh, you are so much more. You are EVERYTHING.

As of today, become transparent.
Disclose to those concerned the secrets gnawing at you and blocking your joy. Because any secret weighs on you, slows you down in your progress.

How to become free of all need when one is continually keeping in the dark a part of himself or of his past?
Move on to action, because this action shall have a repercussion on the rest of humanity. Remember that we are interconnected. The darkness that you personally transcend turns into light for the benefit of others.
Be watchful of this. Observe that when you make a step forward and divulge a secret, society then follows with the same step in the same twinkling of an eye. However incredible it may seem!

I've lived through this miraculous case: A woman friend was sexually abused by her employer. Although it remained a secret to no one, this woman never pressed charges against her aggressor who carried on his work unbothered.
Ten years later, on the very date of her aggression, the young woman put an end to her life. It was on the exact prescribed date of her rape.

This suicide led to a strong surge of awareness in the community. Those who knew about the aggression denounced the guilty boss.

Through her death, the young woman has opened our eyes to the fact that we must not keep silent when we face this type of behavior, no matter what may be the status of the rapist.

A month later the Weinstein case broke out revealing to the whole world the names of many aggressors protected by their high functions.

Everything is connected, everything is in constant interaction.

How to say what you really think without offending or hurting the person you're talking to?

Find out about Non-Violent Communication (NVC).

This method teaches you how to say what you think and feel without having the person you're talking to take it personally, or feel accused, judged or denigrated.

NVC allows you to express clearly your needs in order to have them respected or even fulfilled.

Marshall Rosenberg wrote the first book that treats this subject.

**Release yourself from the need of
controlling your life or that of others.
Release yourself from the habit of hiding, lying or
manipulating in order to obtain what you want,
as you no longer want anything.
Everything is already there.
Everything is perfect.
YOU ARE EVERYTHING.**

STEP 25

You are ageless.

You don't have an age.
Or else you are likely to be as old as the universe!
Because all existing matter was born at the moment of the Big Bang.
"Nothing gets lost, nothing gets created, everything gets transformed", said Lavoisier.

Your conscience has no notion of time. Your physical body does. But the inner observer that is you is not affected by the passage of time.
Your conscience is continuously neutral and changeless. Whether you look at your reflection at three years old or at fifteen or at thirty five or at eighty, it's always with the same eyes of the soul. Only the material body is affected by the passing of years.
Your body is your earthly 'vehicle' that you received for this incarnation.
At birth, the veil of forgetfulness erased from your memory, the countless other lives spent in the past as well as those that you will live in the future.
Because EVERYTHING happens in the present, in the instant, in the absolute, EVERYTHING is.
Our eyes perceive a stone as something fixed and compact, nevertheless it is made up of void and of moving particles: the atoms of rock are in perpetual movement.

It is from now on pointless to celebrate your birthday, because having one more or less year has no more meaning to you. The age of the physical body is a lure from this world of illusions.
Celebrations of this sort reinforce the ego, which should rather tend to disappear with time...
If you wish to make a party with friends, it is useless trying to find a reason other than your wish to see them and to celebrate the Love shining in each one of you.

You must unlearn what you know and forget who you think you are in order to detach yourself from your ego so that it doesn't direct your life anymore, but rather, that it may at last hand you the reins.
Only your soul will be able to guide you towards the best of worlds.
Detach yourself from your personality, by the same token you'll become detached from your sufferings, from your difficult past and your fears related to the future.
If you are all, you have nothing more to fear. Your trust in life shall be complete. Because nothing is outside of you. You are therefore the creator of what happens to you, even if you are not aware of it. Thus, you create what is best for the evolution of your conscience, to incarnate your divine nature on earth.

If you're no one in particular because you are Absolute conscience, so the world can carry on its fancies, with or without you. It's perfect in both cases.
Therefore you are without age, without first name and family name, without children, parent, attachment,

responsibilities, without rights either because you are ALL.
ALL does what its soul tells him to do.
ALL makes unconditional Love say what it is.
You don't have a territory, you're not even human.
It's all an appearance, part of a stage set, an illusion of matter…
Universal Conscience created this life size theater play to learn how to know itself, discover itself, meet its various facets, everywhere and at the same time.

When you look at yourself in the mirror, become conscious that the canal through which you see is as a universal canal! Become aware that EVERYBODY observes through that same canal.
Everyone sees what's around him/her by that unique canal. Understand that your conscience is omnipresent, that others live their lives while being this same 'Universal Conscience'.

You are aware of your earthly experience through what seems to be 'your' conscience, while all the other living beings are also aware of their experience in the same manner.
You don't have any age anymore. Because age and time are an illusion and this, you shall integrate each day a bit more.
You are not that body growing old. You are not that skin getting wrinkles, you are not that person who believes to be inevitably approaching 'death'.

Become aware of this new truth and see how much freedom it confers to you!
Fear ebbs away, ego vanishes as well as susceptibility.
At last, you may live fully, trusting and letting go.
Everything is perfect.

Creativity is the essence of childhood. Manifestly, in our modern society, this creativity as well as imagination are quickly put aside for the benefit of more 'rational and useful' occupations.
Nonetheless, during our whole life, we need to maintain the creativity of our inner child in order to dwell each day in joy and creation.
Such is the secret of eternal youth. The physical age is of no importance as long as our creativity lives and flourishes in us.

People who hope to ward off the aging of the body by remaining 'young' think that it's enough to imitate the lifestyle of a student: party, drinking, have no responsibilities, seduce…
However, student habits don't reflect the best what is the youth of the mind, but rather the creative and spontaneous buzzing of an eight year old child!
By accomplishing all kinds of things (drawing, poetry, music, arts and crafts, fashion design, DIY activities, gardening, dance, singing, physical exercise…), you shall preserve the spark of joy and living that is growing in you each day a bit more.

Release yourself from your need to be attractive.
Freedom from the dictate of being young and beautiful.
Release yourself from the fear of passing time,
of growing old and of death.
Release yourself from the obligation to deny
who you are to attempt to be 'what you should be'.
YOU ARE EVERYTHING.

STEP 26

The illusion of the couple.

Beyond the veil of forgetfulness and the world of illusions, the Universal Conscience took on an earthly body to live out experiences!

When an individual understands and integrates the fact that he isn't this body, but that he is that unlimited, changeless and eternal conscience, it is called the 'Awakening'.
The being who has lived this 'return to the source' will never be the same again. He will have seen, personally seen, without the shadow of a doubt, that he is ALL, that he's creating this world at each instant, that we are all ONE, that we are therefore all interconnected.
He won't doubt anymore because he will have lived this experience in his soul and conscience, from then on, he knows.
The conscience that he is ALL will not therefore be an act of faith, but rather an act of knowledge.
Truly, he understands that it isn't really 'a return to the source' since he never left this source!
He was always in it but had temporarily forgotten.
The 'sleeping' being is hypnotized by this world of appearances which he has gone along with since his physical 'birth'.

As for the couple, once you have perfectly integrated the fact that you are ONE, then you no longer fall in the trappings of egotistical love and passionate love.

Because you know that couples are formed thanks to a hormone which makes you believe that your partner is unique and irreplaceable. This hormone is called **serotonin** and only lasts for a short while. It then gives place to a new sort of relation.
A more peaceful and lucid relation in which the libido is less present, in which we are less blinded by the so-called perfection of the mate. The latters' defaults appear to us. The sharing of daily life allows us to deepen our relationship, our complicity without the cradle of illusions.
After the serotonin, another hormone comes in play, called **oxytocin**.
The latter is not exclusively reserved to couples. Each person (friends, family…) that we love and take in our arms, makes our body to produce oxytocin. At this point may begin a real relation of Unconditional Love.

When we have learned to see beyond the screen of matter, we are no longer duped by this game of seduction and attraction/repulsion, which only comes from our biological organisms, our ego and incarnate personality. And not from our true and deep divine nature.
It's part of the theater play that we are enacting together on this planet.

The myth of the soul mate or twin flame is a lure from which you detach yourself.
It is nothing more than an obstinate allurement, a utopic hope having no more reason to be in a world in which each one is awakening from the sleeping divine within.

Homo Deus is EVERYTHING, why would he need another half?

You are perfect such as you are whether alone or in a couple.

Now, play! Do 'as if' to attract this new reality.

Play at doing as if you had lived the Awakening. Because the Law of Attraction aligns reality to what you think, say and do.

That which is repeated daily, will progressively take root and anchor itself in matter.

Have fun...Imagine: how would you be if you had lived the Awakening?

Starting from this twenty-sixth step, train yourself to think, express and act as if you knew-for having lived it-that you are ALL.

From now on, be Homo Deus!

Become at this precise moment the absolute being that you yearn to be.

In any case, conduct yourself as it would conduct itself.

To know how this divine being would conduct itself, ask yourself:

"How would Unconditional Love act in this situation or with this individual?"

As a reminder: Unconditional Love loves itself as much as it loves others.

Thus, respect yourself in the same manner that you respect others.

Do each day what you aspire to do, what echoes in you.

Don't accept any proposition or situation which makes you feel uneasy or which doesn't match the values incarnated by love.
Don't be 'nice'. Be real, authentic.

I suggest that you read the book *"Being Genuine: Stop Being Nice, Start Being Real"* by Thomas d'Ansembourg.
It allows one to tell apart the difference between saying 'yes' to please others and saying 'yes' when you have really listened to your deepest wish.
It allows you to distinguish between being nice, submitted and obedient from being authentic and master of your own life, while respecting the sovereignty of others.

Being nice is a strength, not a weakness!
Be nice but don't get yourself all tangled up in guilt or empathy for people who use and abuse of it…
Try to remain alert enough to tell the difference between a sincere person and a toxic person playing the victim.

The 'Law of the strongest' rules in this period of survival.
It was established by patriarchy.
On the other hand, the 'Law of collective mutual assistance' is our original mode of life!
Mutual aid and social support originate from the matriarchal system of society.
It's all about 'solidarity'. Here lies the whole difference.

Release yourself from the desperate
search of a soul mate.
Make way for games, experimentation,
lightheartedness and joy.
No longer have fear of death which
prevented you from living your life fully!
YOU ARE EVERYTHING.

STEP 27

You don't 'need' anything anymore to be happy and joyful.

Be joyful, you are joy.
Be at peace and joyful with or without home, with or without meal, with or without lover, with or without family, with or without work, with or without car…
You don't need anything to be, just be.

What you possess or want to possess shall be, sooner or later, the cause of suffering because the joy of obtaining it will give place to the fear of losing it or the sadness of having lost it.
Thus, if you have, it's good. If you don't have, it's good too.
Accept what is, without judging, without putting a positive or negative connotation on it.

Stop wanting to seduce those around you.
Quit being nice, well behaved or perfect just in order to be pleasing.
Listen to yourself, do what you heart yearns after and always act to respect it.
No longer put yourself under any pressure to be attractive, pleasant, kind and cool.
Just be yourself.

During a discussion, don't try to fill silences at all costs. Let your ideas come quietly, without forcing.
Don't give out compliments right and left hoping to be loved or to help the other love himself.
Listen, but don't constrain yourself to when you don't feel like it or when the other party goes on and on.
Speak, but never oblige yourself to talk if the other person doesn't show any sign of interest for you to carry on. Don't be sour over his lack of interest. Don't take it personally.
Let him think what he wants. Let him be interested by nothing other than himself or his problems.
Everything is good.
Nothing bothers you. You accept what is and that's perfect.

"The origin of suffering is attachment. Now the only constant in the universe is change." Buddha said.
To become attached to beings and things is inevitably a source of pain because nothing is changeless in this world.
Change is to be accepted. You must absolutely not fight against change, at the risk of dying from exhaustion.
"Change is not painful, only the resistance to change is so." Buddha also said.
Once again, Buddha is speaking of attachment to an initial situation and a refusal to see it evolve.

Be content with what you have and with who you are.
Let go of your hopes and yearnings which are projected in the future, never in the here and now.
Each moment, accept life such as it is, as it comes.

Practice daily to love who you are, without expecting anything else.
Love yourself as you are, with what you already have.
Love others the way they are.
Be happy without any reason.

Learn to tell the difference between things that you can change and things that are beyond your control.
Act on what depends of you and let go of your expectations for the rest.

Release yourself from the need to possess a spouse, some offspring, a house, trendy shoes, money, expensive clothes, a car, valuable objects…
What you have is perfect. Love it and love yourself.
YOU ARE EVERYTHING.

STEP 28

Cease all struggle within you.

Let go of your desires, your expectations, your hopes, your regrets, your remorse, your wants, your guilt and your fears…
Accept what is, whatever comes, without judgment.

Accomplish your projects and yearnings, without expecting bells and whistles.
Do whatever your heart dictates you to do. Let your mind express its criticisms and fears, without giving it any attention.
Quit fighting for or against things.
All struggle is tiring, exhausting. In addition, any victory will only be short-lived because new conflicts will always reappear.
You have sway over some elements of your existence, but you can't control life in general nor the course of events.
On the other hand, you are master over your letting go!
This is also free will: to decide the manner in which you are going to accept emotionally the situations that occur.
You can cease WANTING to be anything other than what you are now.

Stop wanting to be skinnier, fatter, taller, smaller, more intelligent, prettier, more handsome, younger, more mature, more tanned, richer, more loved, more admired, calmer, more athletic, wiser…

Abandon the desire to be in better health, to be cured, to be more extraverted, to be more this or that.
Because these expectations are eating up your precious energy, deviating it towards sterile suffering.
Your expectations are inner struggles.
Your desires are inner struggles.
Your expectations make you procrastinate.
Your desires make you feel guilty for not succeeding to be or obtaining what you aim for.
How much pointless pain is inflicted upon yourself!
Don't fight against yourself. Love who you are.
Quit fighting for a better world, for a society that is more just. Love the world as it is.
Stop fighting to change a person, to heal another, to relieve so and so, to try preventing someone from doing harm…
Love others such as they are.

Remember that everything is perfect. Everything has a reason to be which you can't perceive or conceive.
You are not to judge the cogwheels of fate.
Neither are you to judge yourself or your surroundings.
When you shall be at peace inside of you, then the outside world will also become so. Because we are INTERCONNECTED: the outside IS the inside, the individual IS the rest of individuals.
They are all connected since they are the same entity.
EVERYTHING is connected to EVERYTHING.
Know that the outside world is only the reflection of your inner world. This society is the mirror of your personal universe.
If you wish for world peace, first find peace within yourself.

Accept each event as it comes.
When you have the power to act on certain elements of your life, then magnify them, transform them into their most beautiful versions.
But for events that are outside of your sphere of action, let go of any emotion and judgment that invades your body and mind. Because these struggles consume energy and are vain.

Concerning events and people on which you have no sway, let them have their own adventures. They are free, just as you are, to experiment the life they have decided to lead.
Give them your trust.
Trust in life.
Trust in yourself.
You have the ability to distinguish between what you can transform and the rest.
Thus is life. Love it for what it is, for what it offers you.
Living this terrestrial adventure is an incalculable chance!

Quit your habit of 'always wanting more and better'.
Be released from your desire of wanting to control
what you feel, what you think, what you want,
what you say and what you are living.
YOU ARE EVERYTHING.

STEP 29

Cease all judgment.

Each one does his best, according to his own vision of the world, according to his own truth.
Neither good nor bad. Just facts.

The reasons which make each event useful for your evolution are beyond your grasp.
The higher goal of the Universe cannot be apprehended by the human brain.
Keep trusting in life because Absolute Conscience knows what it is doing. Everything is perfect.
Take the opportunity to practice the cessation of all judgment, of others and also of yourself.
The task is enormous, but it is beautiful.

Love without judging.
Accept people the way they are.
Receive others with their attitudes without categorizing them.
Cease to criticize the comings, goings and sayings of everyone.
Abandon all your judgments about different kinds of cultures or religions.

Because all judgment induces suffering: you suffer to see someone acting 'badly', you cry hearing about such or such an
account or action which you deem to be 'horrible'.

In parallel, you spread negative thoughts around you, while it is joy and love that needs to radiate.

When you face 'unpleasant' or 'sad' events, learn to focus on your body's sensation in the present moment. Let go of negative thoughts, they only nourish your suffering.

Thus, you can transcend the difficulty and recover your inner peace, your original and timeless joy.

Your soul judges nothing nor anyone, not even yourself. Because it is pure and absolute Love.

It is only your mind which seeks to put people into categories, into boxes of 'nice' or 'mean'.

When in fact, our Homo Deus evolution places the soul above all else and leaves the ego in the background.

The mind is ideal to help you organize the practicalities of your terrestrial life.

The mind is perfect to manage, count, classify and materialize. It has great practical and logical value. But it isn't there to direct your life!

Only your conscience knows and loves all, even though it only reveals to you a few items at a time.

Have faith in it, you can trust it blindly, without condition and expectation.

Accept to do what your soul dictates you to do and then entrust to your mind the task of accomplishing it. But don't allow it to have any say as to whether it's a good idea or not! Your mind doesn't know, it doesn't understand the Great All. Your conscience does, because your conscience IS Universal conscience.

From now on, make abstraction of 'you', i.e. the filter through which you look at, comment and judge what happens.

If you are no longer identified to your personality of flesh, then you no longer have an opinion to make about the behavior of others. You are the other, so you allow your fellows to act as they see fit.

You are them. You are thus happy to be able to experiment 'your' own choices and to assume the consequences of 'your' own decisions.

You don't need to hate or punish an action or human being which you find 'reprehensible'.

The universe in its perfection shall take care of it. The Law of Attraction operates as 'divine justice' because 'as you sow thus shall you reap'.

As for those who propagate Love, they shall reap the fruits of love.

Although you are to pay attention to your actions, nonetheless, don't judge them!

Trust yourself. Do your best.

Correct your thoughts, your speech and your acts as soon as you understand that they don't bear joy or peace.

Step aside in order to become a neutral and loving observer. You are an observer because, in truth, you are the Universal Conscience observing through your eyes.

Love the world as it is because your thoughts are creative!
Therefore, create beauty and love rather than criticism and judgment.

As a test proof, let us consider Masaru Emoto, the scientist who studied water (see step 12).
Masaru did an experiment on the influence of thought on rice:
He placed some rice in three different pots.
Then he stuck labels on each pot; he noted 'Love' on the first pot, 'Hate' on the second, and 'Indifference' on the third.
Each time he passed in front of these pots, he said kind and positive words to the first pot, injurious and negative words to the second, as for the third pot, he completely ignored it.

This experiment proved after a few weeks, that the rice in the pot with 'Love' was far better conserved than the one with 'Indifference'.
On the other hand, the contents of the pot with 'Hate' were rotting even more than the one with 'Indifference'…

Thus, always give a kind look to yourself, others and life in general.
Love yourself. Spread thoughts of peace and harmony. Because in the invisible world, the vibration which you emit is capable of transforming everything, even matter that is most dense.

Avoid watching war movies, or horror and gory films. The attention you give them nourishes the low energy that animates them.
In addition, it will be very hard being joyful after watching an anguishing or morbid film for two hours…

As much as you can, always choose light, happiness and Love.

Release yourself from the habit of criticizing, commenting, judging, analyzing everything around you, ranging from the weather to reproaches from a neighbor…
Free yourself from the habit of suffering when facing events which you classify as being unpleasant.
YOU ARE EVERYTHING.

STEP 30

Become a breatharian.
Drink water, fruit juices without pulp,
vegetable broths without any solids in suspension.

You no longer need to drink nourishing fruit juices.
Just a glass of water and the splendor of life will flow in you.

In your innermost being, you know that you ARE life itself.
You alternate between herbal teas, pulp-less or diluted fruit juices and vegetable broths. You have perfectly integrated, beyond the shadow of a doubt, the fact that you are the energy of Love experimenting itself in matter. Thus you feed yourself with inner light.
You know that you are All. You are vibration.
Everything is energy (subtle/invisible and dense/visible) and there is only one source of energy: pure Love.

I suggest that you re-read step 12, which talks about water and its amazing properties. This will motivate you further to overcome obstacles.

With the effects of global warming, temperatures in general are on the rise. A more basic, light, aqueous and raw diet is more suitable in these conditions.
Notice that during the summer, you naturally want fresh juices, sherbets, tabboulleh, salad or fruit salads.

Whereas in the winter, you would rather have a hot chocolate, a stew, a gratin or warm dishes that are rich in fat.
The planet and its inhabitants are raising their vibration in unison.
Thus, the planet is evolving. It is cleansing and purifying itself. It is transcending its darkness and duality towards a more unified version of itself.
In the same way, we are being led to transform ourselves.

Global warming is quite real, nevertheless, it isn't to be blamed on humans.
True, multinational companies have wrecked biodiversity and polluted lands and seas. However, this has nothing to do with temperature change.
Inform yourself on the subject. You will find that the sun has cycles which follow one another, like our seasons on earth.
Nowadays, the sun is in a hotter phase. This becomes obvious when you realize that the temperatures are also rising on the other planets of our solar system!
Everything evolves. Everything is born, grows, dies and is born again. The only constant is change.
Thus it has been with dinosaurs, mammoths, dodos, saber tooth lions…
Thus it is today with whales, pandas and innumerable other endangered species.
Everything has meaning, everything is perfect. Death is only an illusion, just as life is.
The medias are pushing to an extreme our responsibility in this so-called ecological disaster because it raises us one against the other. It frightens us, then divides us.

We then become an incredibly docile society, a population ready to accept the freedom impeding laws and to implore for 'protection' against events which frighten us.

This is the objective of all this ecological and climatic mystification.

Therefore, toss your guilt away and concentrate on the reason for your presence here:

Your personal evolution, growing in conscience.

Gaia, our planet, is sovereign and doesn't need us to be saved.

It isn't a victim, just like you're not a poor powerless victim either.

Everything is in perfect correlation with the plan of evolution which we have come to experiment on earth.

Let us remember this and act accordingly.

Dr. Patrick Moore said: *"the environmental movement has become the most powerful source there is to hamper the flourishing of developing countries. (...) I think it is legitimate for me to qualify it as 'anti-human'. "*

Always listen to your body and your conscience. If one or the other refuses or doesn't seem ready to accomplish this step, listen to it and respect its choice!

Remember that there mustn't be any inner or outer conflict.

EVERYTHING in you must tend towards the accomplishment of this new step. If there is the least reluctance or resistance, it means that you must remain patient and work more deeply on the preceding steps.

You can also go on to the following steps, while remaining continually vigilant of your feelings to identify the right moment when you will be ready to incarnate the breatharian phase.

Be in harmony. Don't impose anything to your body, if not you would just be playing the game of illusions and obligations.
Bear in mind that you will always continue to 'nourish' yourself. You are not fasting yet you are no longer eating solid food. You are nourished by Universal Love, by prana, this light vibrating within and around you.
Eating consists in swallowing physical foods to nourish a physical body. Whereas 'feeding yourself in conscience' is an act of total freedom!
You can choose between eating physical nutrients, and the subtle energy called 'prana' or Absolute Love of which you are completely made up of.
It's a decision that you can take and take over again at each moment of your life. There is no radicalism or exclusivity to be maintained.

Keep on listening within yourself and remain fluid. Surf on the possibilities which life presents to you. Take the time to question yourself when a new proposal comes up.
You are free to choose the way you want to feed yourself.

When your conscience gives you the signal, abandon pulpous fruit juices and thick vegetable juices.
Ask each day your physical body in order to hear its needs and wishes.
Don't allow your fear to take control on your diet. Trust yourself.

Drink as much water as you want. As explained in step 12, have fun vitalizing and informing water by laying your hands around it or by creating a vortex (when there's a whirlpool, it stores the information you give to it).
Drink as much herbal tea, light broths and diluted fruit juices as wanted.
You are your own master.

If you feel the need to eat a more substantial meal or a richer beverage, allow yourself to do it. Don't become a dictator to yourself. Love yourself and respect yourself.
Thus, little by little, you'll attain the state of a breatharian. That is to say, one who nourishes himself solely from water, light juices and lump-less broths.

Here are examples of personalities who fed themselves **only with water** (or a daily host) during weeks, months or years:
Marthe Robin (1902-1981), Therese Neumann (1898-1962), Alexandrina de Balazar (1904-1955), Jasmin Herrera, Michael Werner (author of the book *"Life from Light: Is it Possible to Live without Food? - A Scientist Reports on His Experiences")*, Henry Montfort drinks only water since 2002…
Since 1995, Hira Ratan Manek nourishes herself only with solar light and solarized water (exposed to sun during eight hours).
Gaston Bacchiani feeds himself solely with water and certain other liquids since 2013.
Ivan Orlic is a scientist who experimented the '11 day process' with Victor Truviano and the '21 day process'

with Nicolas Pilartz. Today, Ivan continues his exploration of pranism by studying several breatharians.

Emeya S. Angelism did her first '21 day process' in 2013, followed by 13 months of a water-based diet with an occasional addition of honey (four times) in the water.

The 21 day process (and also the 11 day one) is a course animated by a pranic person. It accompanies one during the transition between eating material food and a pranic diet.

Michael Werner and Hira Ratan Manek were validated by modern scientists because they accepted to submit themselves to an uninterrupted medical observation during several weeks.

**Release yourself from the need to
drink substantial juices and thick soups.
Be free from your belief of having to
eat physical food to stay alive, it's a lie.
You get closer each day a bit more to a pranic diet.
YOU ARE EVERYTHING.**

STEP 31

You are no longer sad for people that you have lost, whether they be dead or still alive.

You are not sad anymore for people alive who are suffering.
Because you know for sure in the bottom of your heart that they are all eternal and made of Pure Love.
Their bodies are temporary, but their soul has no beginning nor ending, like yours.
If it is possible for you to help them and stop their suffering, then do it.
On the other hand, if their problem lies outside of your realm of action, then remember that they are master of their own lives and that their conscience has created this experience for their evolution.

You were never separated from them. We are the same Universal Conscience, the same entity.
Just as you cease to identify yourself to your human persona, so you also cease to thus identify others by narrowing them to their simple earthly envelope.
Remember that they are living an enriching experience.
They are not only individuals that you see in matter. Their essence is immortal.
Thus, they have the choice to incarnate each day either Love or fear.

If the absence of a being is heavy to you, it's that need which you must learn to accept, to love and to transcend.

You have no need to be sad for him, because he chose his fate before being born on this planet.
Furthermore, he is following his path on other levels.
Everything is perfect.

The deceased person is not a poor victim. He/she is sovereign, like you.
In truth, there is neither persecutor nor victim. Each person attracts the situation that is necessary to wake his conscience up and that of his surroundings.
Your soul is the creator of your life and will not spare you any event that will help you grow in conscience. You may trust yourself. What happens is masterfully orchestrated in the perspective of living the most beautiful adventure: to incarnate Love in matter!
An abundance of heightening experiences are leading you on the path of personal fulfilment, on the way of the Homo Deus evolution.
Without value judgment, accept what cannot be changed. Then accept the emotions running through you. Don't fight against them. They are precious and necessary.
They only pass through you and will not remain forever.
These emotions are not you. Love them when they occur and learn not to be their prisoner. Let them disappear naturally.

In some cases, your suffering is really 'reassuring'…you know it by heart and it seems to define you.
But it only defines the egotistic individual presently incarnated. That individual is not you.
You are Love. You are pure conscience. Your energy vibrates at a higher frequency.

Each person plays his part wonderfully in this theater play that is life.

The bad are awfully bad, the good are beautifully nice.

In each one of us, there is good and beauty but also hate and violence.

In the end, we are the materialization of an energy of absolute Love.

Universal Conscience has become dense to the extreme in order to be able to take part in this illusory comedy, of which one of the goals is to always learn yet a bit more about itself, to experiment itself.

Conscience laughs, cries, loves, tears itself up, hates itself, forgives itself, finds itself again, rises in the conscience of itself...

Nevertheless, these experiences have never existed elsewhere than in the bosom of this encompassing Conscience. Everything happens in its 'imagination' that is so powerful that we all believe in it.

When you dream, observe your feeling: during the dream, you are convinced that it is real!

Your emotions and sensations are as real as when you are awake.

Thus is it for this existence.

Accept what is. And welcome whatever you feel when facing what is.

Let go, while pursuing your path with faith in the future and trust in yourself. Because you are its creator. Each of your choices, each of your thoughts, of your actions, will orient your future in one way or another.

So smile and love what you are, without judging yourself, without demanding the best in all and for all.

When you see someone who is suffering, if you can help him, help him tenderly, without forcing.
Make sure that he does want you to help him…
However, if you can't rescue him, because he chooses not to receive your help or he prefers to experiment his belief, his fear or his decision, then let go.
It is no longer your responsibility.

Remember that he is free. That he is the creator of his life. That he is the master of the body and soul which he received when he was born. It's his choice.
If you feel pain in observing his suffering, then love yourself.
Give yourself Love.
Greet, appease and love the trouble rising in you. Don't allow this emotion to dominate you.
You are not this emotion, it just passes by you.
Don't keep it persistently in your thoughts, words or actions.

If you have lost someone that is important to you, then love yourself and accept your sadness. Let this sadness run through your body and mind, however put a stop to it after a few minutes.
Thus, it won't anchor itself in you. Because your body of flesh needs your energy to carry on its path.

If you miss the deceased person, think about him and speak to him as though he were still there.
Know that he has never really left you. He will hear you if you call him.
Death is as much of an illusion as life is…

**Freedom from your need to place a border between the visible world and the invisible/subtle worlds.
Be released from your belief of having been or of being separated from people who are deceased because, actually, you were never far from them.
They are still there, transformed, different, but you are always connected.
You are them and they are you.
YOU ARE EVERYTHING.**

STEP 32

In this world of illusion, everything is in perpetual movement. On the other hand, in Reality, nothing ever changes.

Everything is in movement: even the stone, the rock and the mountain!
Modern science has allowed us to discover the existence of tiny particles called 'atoms'. Although invisible to the naked eye, atoms are in perpetual movement.
As these atoms make up everything, which physically exists, we can conclude that everything is in movement, even if it is imperceptible.

However, there does exist **ONE changeless thing** because it is timeless. It is the energy which is the cornerstone of the universe, I have stated: "the Love vibration".
This timeless energy is permanent. It is everywhere, at all times.
Thus, be reassured, you don't risk anything! You can discard your fear of death, your fear of disappearing because it is IMPOSSIBLE. You are. And you shall be for eternity.
There where you really are, there is neither beginning nor end. Neither movement nor stillness.
You are this omnipresent all, this great ALL.
Your fleshly body has a limited timespan but that body isn't you!

In the earthly time-space continuum, put yourself also in movement: allow your creativity to express itself, become an admirer of the world around you, love it.
Observe and thank the beauty of a landscape, of a smile, a flower, a face, a starry sky.
Become Love by being subjugated by the esthetics which this incarnation offers you.
Surround yourself with colors, with harmonious melodies, songs, nature, art, physical activity, with all kinds of creations and handiwork.

Be in the abundance of creativity when it comes to materializing an idea.
Be in a state of grace when your body and the dexterity of your fingers allow you to write, to cook, to repair a broken object, to garden, to play an instrument, to perform a play, to dance, to sing…
Create, invent, vibrate and love!
Become a child again with an exuberant imagination.
Be playful, light, in the present moment, be happy to be there, master of your body and time.
Love is the energy that creates.
Imitate Love and create in turn beauty, health, equity and brotherhood.

Everything is moving, everything is change.
Everything is creation, evolution, transformation and perfection.
Inspiration is sent to you directly by your soul, i.e. by the Universal Conscience.

Your intuition is due to an intimate connection with your soul. Yearn to receive its messages, it's a mind blowing gift!
Become the actor of your life, generate the harmony that is around you each day.
The body that you have is a priceless jewel! Use it well. Make it live, make it move, dance, juggle, run…
This body is a precious tool which you must maintain and feed with beauty from all areas!
Remember that you have come to experiment on this planet precisely that which 'you' are not: mortal and in constant movement.
In truth, you are immortal and changeless.
You have always existed and will always exist.

Train yourself to visualize the world around you in a new way: everywhere you lay your eyes, imagine that they only see a succession of rotating particles, like tiny specks of luminous dust orbiting around their central nucleus.
Look through the filter of a mega-giga-microscope…

Thus you shall not see a chair on a tiled floor, but an infinity of atoms spinning on themselves.
When you look at yourself in the mirror, transcend this image. See beyond your appearance. Admire the colored vibration which composes you. See how it is teems with waves of pure Love!

For this step, you must go beyond the reality which you think that you know. Learn to see in a new way with the eyes of Universal Conscience. Everything is code and energy.

The theater of illusion in which you live is not made up of solid and changeless matter.

It's in fact a fluid substance perpetually in movement!

Be interested in quantum physics.

Nassim Haramein is a Swiss scientist physicist, specialized in quantum mechanics.

He founded a new theory which shook the scientific world: the theory of unified fields.

Nassim maintains, among other things, that space is not made of void. It has an electromagnetic structure measurable on Planck's scale (i.e. the smallest scale there is).

In other words, void is not void. It 'seems' void to us when in fact, it is constituted of tiny elements…

We are therefore surrounded by invisible particles which connect us to the rest of the world!

According to him, primordial energy is the source of the physical world. What we consider to be void, in opposition to solid matter, is full of energy, and this energy, rich in information, connects everything.

From that the fact arises that we are all interconnected!

Freedom from your belief of being fragile, vulnerable and mortal.
Your actual physical body is so, but your soul, your pure essence is changeless.
Be free from procrastination. Act and live.
YOU ARE EVERYTHING.

STEP 33

Only Love exists.

Think of **the person you love**, admire or respect the most.
Whoever it may be, consider all the Love and adoration you consecrate to this person.
Feel the warmth of this energy.
Now imagine that in reality, this wonderful being that you idolize, is you!

Is it Buddha? Is it Jesus Christ? Is it your mother? Is it a writer? A passed away singer? A painter? A mathematical genius?
Whoever it may be, when you look at this person, in the absolute, it's you that you love and contemplate. And it's beautiful.
You are he. He is you.
It's the most luminous, the most brilliant and the most marvelous part that is in you.
Feel the unlimited power of Love that you are capable of giving him.
This Love, offer it to yourself as well.

You free will is the repeated choice, at each moment, of taking the path of Love OR the path of fear. You always have this choice, for every situation in life.
Thus, starting today, create your life by following the way of the heart.

To do this, make silence within you. Appease your mind. Walk or meditate with eyes closed in order to hush your inner monolog.

Then, when your emotions are neutral, when your thoughts run without attaching any importance to them, listen to your wants, listen to the subtle yearnings which Love dictates to you.

Incarnate joy, raise your vibration in order to arrive at the high level of pure and great ideas.

There, when the right action seems clear to you, then take the decision to follow it and materialize it at that moment.

Don't put it off till tomorrow.

Don't wait for help from the outside, nor for an ulterior validation. No. Go for it!

If you ignore what meaning to give to your life, if you believe everything is vain, that all is doomed, then accomplish the only mission which is important: LOVE.

Love yourself, love the other, love life, love people, the planet, the sky, animals…

LOVE, again and always, from morning to night.

If you love, then your life will be full and flourishing.

If you have loved, your life will have been sublime and authentic!

Only Love is real. Only love counts.

Experiment love in all of its forms, in all areas, from the most subtle to the densest. Love is universal, omnipresent and eternal.

It's simple and essential. Nevertheless, loving seems so difficult in this society in which love has been discredited to the point of being made ridiculous.

Know for a fact that the modern world functions upside down.

Today, values are inverted.

Films and media advocate glory, power, youth, individuality, egocentrism and wealth at the expense of others, women that are fragile, vulnerable and desirable, men that are insensitive, unwavering and virile…

Stars are fascinatingly narcissistic. They are praised for the outer beauty, their charismatic appearance, their shallowness, their indecent opulence, their eternal youth and their exacerbated thinness.

But, we are aligned with our soul when we dwell in truth, sincerity, authenticity, maturity, wisdom, humility, sharing, equity, uninterested friendship and unconditional love.

In other words, the exact opposite of the values promoted by our society!

At each moment of your life, ask yourself this question:
"What would Love do in my situation?"

What would Love do about this person, but also, what would Love do about me?

Do you love yourself by adopting this behavior? Do you love your neighbor when talking to him this way? Do you love life while neglecting it in this manner?

Now that you know this 'key', you just need to apply it each day in every situation.

Be lucid enough to observe your behavior.

Aim for your highest aspirations.

Once you are on the path of Love, be certain that the universe will favor your projects!
Thus, it will send you help and the necessary synchronicities to live at best this terrestrial experience.
The universe will support you since the universe is you. There is nothing outside of you. You are ALL.
It's a virtuous circle:
When you follow the path indicated by your conscience (which is none other than Love), you are perfectly aligned with your soul. By the same token, this harmony will sustain your joy each day. This joy will increase your vibration. Now when you vibrate in Love, you are situated at such heights that everything flows with fluidity and grace!
Events follow one another in an absolutely perfect manner. And the basis of this virtuous circle is to keep an absolute faith in life. Therefore in you.

All the futures remain possible and feasible at each moment.

To understand that an inevitable and fixed future is not a fatality, it is enough to look at the Chladni 'figures'.
Chladni has highlighted the perfection of vibrations thanks to a thin metallic plate sprinkled with white sand.
By maintaining this plate in a perfect balance, he made a bow vibrate on one of its extremities.
Immediately, symmetric and geometric shapes appeared on the surface, drawn in an ephemeral fashion by the grains of sand.

These sketches would radically change at the least variation of the rubbing of the bow.
Thus is the universe, all events can occur as soon as you change the vibration!

**Be released from your belief of being
overwhelmed by fear, hate or need.
Freedom from the illusion of believing
that you are not pure and absolute love.
In truth, only Love exists.
The rest is just an illusion
which allows this Love
to experiment itself again and always.
YOU ARE EVERYTHING.**

STEP 34

About forgiveness.

Think of **the person that you hate the most** in this world. Whether this person is still alive or has existed in the past, think about this individual and become conscious that this hated being…is you.

The hate that you vow to this person, is in fact a hate that you send to yourself!
This individual represents your dark, suffering, fearful and negative part, which you reject.
Yes, you hide a part of yourself because it is easier to think of yourself as nice and exemplary.
You would prefer to veil your face rather than accept your faults, your baseness and your vulnerability.
You don't want to hold a grudge against yourself, even less to feel guilty. On the opposite, congratulate yourself for having at last understood this truth! It is never too late to transform oneself.
Thus, this hated enemy is you. You are him, he is you.
Look at him with as much Love as that which you gave to the loved being in the last step.

Forgiveness is an illusion.
Remember that there is neither persecutor, nor victim, nor savior.
Everything is perfect and necessary to evolve.
Your soul is building you an ideal human life to make you grow in conscience.

Everything is One. You are EVERYTHING.
You are the 'persecutor', you are the 'victim', you are the 'savior'. However, these roles are allurements from the world of illusions.
We 'play' in a script interpreted by majestic souls who wear a 'costume' of darkness during the lapse of an incarnation.
We are all loved and infinitely worthy of Love.
We are all born from the same energy, at various stages of evolution, at different levels of consciousness.
The most difficult is to forgive yourself of your own weaknesses, of your own mistakes. As soon as you manage to, then you will also succeed to 'forgive' those who have hurt you, even if forgiveness is an illusion that is inherent to this comedy that is life.

Everything has a reason to be, which our intellect cannot fathom so much that the divine plan is in fact wide and unmeasurable.
Actually, once you detach yourself from your past, you no longer feel the need to forgive those who have harmed you. Because this past doesn't concern you anymore. You are a new being at each moment.
Once you distance yourself from your personality and ego, it isn't necessary anymore to forgive your mistakes nor those of others nor the so called 'injustices' of the world.
You are the Creator and the creature. There is neither scission nor separation. Just One.
By letting go of the past and de-identifying yourself from your mind and egocentric person, it allows to go beyond pain, regrets, and suffering inflicted by others or yourself.
This distance is the key to inner well-being.

Stay in the present moment.

Thus, the past will no longer come to haunt you, nor will the suffering that you endured by the alleged 'fault' of others.

If thoughts of a situation in which you thought to be the victim come to your mind, love yourself and lay your attention on bodily sensations. Observe your breath, listen to your surroundings, feel the contact of the elements on your skin. Meditate. Do yoga.

Thus the ego of your incarnate person will fade to reveal your real identity: you are the pure energy of Love.

To help go beyond this stage, you can also practice Ho'oponopono (see step 7). It will allow you to become conscious that YOU are the persecutor as much as the victim. Thus the veil of illusion will drop.

We are all connected because we are ONE.

Have you noticed that human relationships always revolve around three roles?

We are rarely neutral with respect to our spokesperson...

In turn, we play the role of the innocent victim of a situation or person. Then that of the savior. And sometimes we also become the persecutor of a situation or person...

It's the famous triangle of Karpman:
> *'Savior-Victim-Persecutor'*

None of these three roles are beneficial because they are always in the trap of illusion.

No, you are never a victim, nor a persecutor, nor a savior!

If you seem to be a victim, it is because your soul has created this situation to accelerate the evolution of your conscience. Same thing for the persecutor or savior.
Let us now put aside this ancestral pattern and take a tangent. Let us cease to endorse each of these three roles!

As a Homo Deus, you have perfectly integrated the fact that chance doesn't exist and that events, which occur to you, are the fruit of your creation for the unique purpose of your evolution.
Every victim has consciously or unconsciously 'authorized' his state and situation in order to learn more about himself, to assert himself and come out of the manipulator/predator stronghold, to manage to transcend his egotistical role.
Every persecutor is also learning about himself.
A little reminder concerning 'narcissistic perverts' which are a type of persecutor which must be avoided at all costs (see step 15). Even if they are 'you' since you are all, they will not change during this incarnation. Your personal challenge will be to assert yourself by definitely getting away from their toxic stronghold.
The fact of knowing that we are all ONE must not incite you to throw yourself into the lion's den or under the wheels of a car…Love always guides you towards life, towards joy.
Love the persecutor but don't remain in his path.
Love the victim, but don't drown yourself with him if he refuses to be helped.
Love yourself, but may your ego not be dependent on the need to save others.

Freedom from your need to be forgiven.
Release from your need to forgive
those who have mistreated you.
Be released from your belief to be different
from the person you hate. That person is you.
Be free from the illusion of not being the person
you admire or love the most in the world.
That person is also you.
YOU ARE EVERYTHING.

STEP 35

Transcend your ego.

You are neither a woman nor a man.
You are neither young nor old.
You are nobody's son or daughter.
You are nobody's brother or sister.
You are no one because you are ALL. You are everyone.
You have nothing to prove. The simple fact of being here and now on this earth makes you legitimate.
Be PRESENT.
You are the incarnation of the Universal Conscience.
You are all the humans present on this earth.
You are all the humans who have lived on this earth
You are all the humans who will live on this earth.
You are all the sensitive beings, alive, having lived and who will live on this earth.
You are all the plants, minerals, elements, alive, having lived and who will live on all the planets of this universe, multiverses and omniverses.
You are the hair flowing in the breeze of the wind.
You are the wind, the pollen, the bird, the cloud that is forming, deforming and reforming without cease.
Love and respect all persons, all animals, all plants because it is yourself that you love and respect by doing this.
Remember that you are the other.

As Jesus said:
"Do to others as you would have them do to you." (Luke 6:31)

When you are no longer the individual that you believe to be in appearance, then you are free from his fears, his needs, his relationship to his family, entourage, job...
Be kind and respectful to those who are kind and respectful to you.
If certain people denigrate you, insult you or hurt you, then depart from them.
Don't seek revenge, don't reprimand them and don't give them a lecture. No. Let them deal with their choices and the consequences of their choices.
If some people are toxic to you, then flee their malevolence. Don't try to either support them at the expense of your own health nor to punish them.
Because helping someone who didn't ask you anything is vain and useless.
And helping someone who continually asks for your assistance, someone who begs for you to stay at his side while not evolving from the start, someone who promises to become better and keeps falling back in his old ways, all of this will only empty you of your energy without even being of any help.
Each person must follow his own path.
You are responsible of your path and of your choices. You are not responsible of those of others.
Let them learn, let them grow in conscience at their own pace.

After all, there must be some place where conscience can incarnate itself to experiment in matter. A place where duality can take place in order to allow souls to evolve.

And this place, is our planet (for example, because there must be other planets).

The Earth, called Gaia of its real name, has volunteered to welcome souls in search of training.

The Earth is conscious of its choice, it isn't a victim and we are not its persecutors!

Everything is perfect and everything is teaching.

It is because Gaia loves us with unconditional Love that it offers itself thus for the rising of our consciousness.

Just like the animals and the plants who love us with such a great love accept to offer themselves for us.

In fact, YOU ARE this earth, YOU ARE the animal and YOU ARE the plant. You offer this gift to yourself.

Thank yourself, thank everything.

Take care of your evolution, listen to your yearnings.

Love humans enough to return to them their total sovereignty. Love them enough to recognize that they are free to experiment that which they have chosen.

Love them with an Absolute Love which accepts to make them responsible and autonomous, even if, in appearance, it seems to go against their happiness or that of others.

If you protect them in spite of themselves, they won't learn. They won't be able to understand from their mistakes.

Trust them.

Know that you are them in the past. That they are you in the future.
That everything happens in the present moment.
Everything coexists.

Train yourself to be detached from what others think about you.
Train yourself to act under the guidance of Love and not through the filter of your personality.
Detach yourself from the many roles that you have endorsed until now.
Act according to your conscience and the deep understanding that you are ALL because you are permanently interacting with yourself and with the multitude of facets of yourself.

Do you adore your parents? Perfect, go on seeing them and loving them. Just become conscious that you are doing it because you want to and have a real affection for them. Not through obligation or by duty. In fact, you can cease to call them 'Dad' or 'Mom' because this sets up a hierarchy, a relation which calls for a certain code of conduct.

Do you love your children? Fine, continue your relation with them. But consider them as beings in their own right, they are sovereign and responsible for their choices. Don't see them as offspring which owe you respect and obeisance. Your children can decide to call you 'Mom' or 'Dad'. But they are in no case obliged to.

Do you love to be surrounded by friends and acquaintances? Perfect. Don't change this habit, as long as you feel free to be with them or not. And that you are authentic in your relation with them and their expectations. Abandoning the mirages of the ego doesn't mean that you must be alone or cut yourself off from your fellow men. On the opposite, love them with Unconditional Love, without expecting anything in return.

**Be released from your need to identify yourself
to the physical person that you are presently.
Free yourself from the need to be someone
in particular, someone special,
someone who is worthy to be loved,
and someone who is worthy to be admired.
All of this is an allurement of the ego.
YOU ARE EVERYTHING.**

STEP 36

The importance of silence and of all the answers it contains.

You have nothing left to do. **You no longer have the 'need' to speak** or to express yourself.
Stop justifying yourself, of having to explain, convince, construct and argument.
Everything is already there. Everything has already been done.

Have you ever listened to someone without interruption although you were in complete disagreement with his remarks? If you manage to let the other end his expression of view, it shows that you have respect for his opinion even though it is at odds with yours.
Thus you allow all differences to exist. And you don't feel "aggressed" by what doesn't match your view.

Speech is never clear or precise enough to reveal who you really are.
One day, language will become superfluous. Because the essential will be evident, one look will be enough to make oneself understood or to grasp a situation.
Silence is powerful, it contains all the answers to all the questions.
EVERYTHING is contained in **Silence**!
Silence is inner peace. Silence is the quietness of the body and the calm of the soul.

Real silence lets the mind speak alone. Your attention is no more focused on that ceaseless monolog.
Words can be misleading, violent and manipulative. They are created by the mind and the ego.
Love doesn't need any words or explanations.
The sound of the voice interrupts the peace of the mind. The flow of words distracts the spirit away from permanent meditation.
To comment on a beautiful landscape, is to categorize it. When it should be enough to allow beauty impregnate you as your eyes are wide open on this wonder.
Self-evidence is not explainable, it is limpid.
Speech highlights the fear of silence. While in fact, silence is our ally!
When we want to avoid silence at all costs whenever we are with one or more persons, we will have the tendency to speak either to say nothing, to speak badly of someone, or to give importance to the superficial and the useless, instead of allowing silence to grow in our presence.
The fear of silence reflects that of the vacuity of our being. When in fact these two fears are allurements. Our silence is full and our being is wealthy of everything.

Experiment silence when you are with someone. Be at peace, let go of the stress which could overcome you when you say nothing. Look inside of you and greet the emotions running through you.
Smile if your heart tells you to smile.
Remember that you are not 'only' that incarnated individual who thinks that his life is played each moment. No. Your true self is immortal and changeless.
Listen to the silence.

Silence will be penetrated by the voice of your soul, of your conscience, that omniscient, omnipresent voice which knows all.

You can experiment silence also in your home as soon as conditions permit. Without music, nor radio nor a lit TV in the background...
Nowadays, silence has become a luxury. It is practically non-existent in our cities. The noise of cars, passersby, ambulances, planes or neighbors is constant.

You may experiment by walking in nature. The silence of the sea, the forests or countryside is vivifying, energizing and nourishing!
Of course, it isn't an absolute silence because the noise of waves, the chirping of birds and the quivering of tree leaves or the hum of insects is present outside. Nevertheless, those sounds are beneficial to health.

As Marshall Rosenberg said, you must choose between *"being happy or being right"!*

**Be released from your need to speak, convince, justify your choices, your actions, your longings.
Freedom from the habit of speaking
all the time, to fill blanks.
Release from your need to avoid
'the passing of an angel' at all costs.
Be free from your belief that silence
represents void, boredom or death.
YOU ARE EVERYTHING.**

STEP 37

Solitude!
Forty days in the desert, alone,
face to face with oneself.

Learn to love yourself, to love being only with yourself.
Learn to spend more time alone, to appreciate silence, calm, inner peace.
Resource yourself far from the city, from the frantic agitation of big towns.
You don't 'have to' be alone imperatively, but you can without any hassle.
Don't avoid others voluntarily.
On the other hand, don't do everything to be with others.
Don't flee from solitude.

In the case of Jesus, the awakening of his divinity was completed in the desert when he was alone for forty days. But solitude was already a part of his life before that. He often walked alone. He meditated each day.
When he faced some difficulty and that an answer was expected of him, a reaction, some guidance, Jesus would sit on the floor and trace circles with a stick…
It was his manner of making emptiness, of discarding sterile thoughts from the mind and leaving the place for luminous ideas to emerge.
He would then reveal what Love had dictated him during his silent introspection. Happy is the loner, because he has gone beyond the compulsory need of always being in the

company of others. Happy is the solitaire because he is released from his fear of being alone.
Happy is the solitaire because he really has the choice between being alone or accompanied.

A human is so made that after a few days of solitude and silence, his brain will create 'imaginary' friends.
We are highly sociable individuals. Which is why we can't bear solitude.
If we remain cut off too long from our fellows, our mind will make some presences to 'appear', spirits, beings, which hold us company.
The mind also has the option of 'giving life' to objects or plants by communicating with them.
Are they a product of our imagination or are they real entities that we perceive through these extreme conditions? Each person will form his own opinion.
EVERYTHING will be conceived by your brain to avoid to your spirit feeling alone with itself!
But nonetheless, it is in that face to face with yourself, in this moment of truth, in this omnipresent silence that is found the conscience of who you really are.

Welcome, love and go beyond the fear of having a long interview with your soul.
When you will have got the taste of being in your own company, then you will have been freed from your need to be with someone. At each moment you can decide to be alone or accompanied.
You will be able to be really objective concerning your friends. You will no longer have to accept toxic people who have felt a lack of confidence in you and are about to

boost it in exchange of their own conditions, more often for their own interests rather than yours…

In addition, you are never really alone because you have a whole universe to discover in you and around you!
Do you have the impression of being a prisoner of your thoughts? To not be able to escape from the infernal cycle of your mental ruminations? It's false. Within you are happening an infinity of activities which you can lay your attention on: your breathing, your heartbeat, the sensation of your clothes on your skin, the smells detected by your nostrils, the asperity of your palate, and sounds, even very faint, which reach your ears…
The silence which vibrates and screams inside of you is also to be perceived.
The omniscience of your conscience, in you, outside of you and outside of time is what among other things you will attain when you are no longer troubled by having to face yourself.

Each day, spend some time alone.

Walk in nature or outside.
Be alone in your room, in your apartment, in your country home, in a hotel, in a foreign country…

Being alone doesn't mean to strictly see no one. This also includes the fact of being surrounded by unknown people, to cross a walker and his dog in a park, to go to the movie theater unaccompanied, to swim in a municipal swimming pool, to visit a crowded museum…

Welcome this solitude as and when it presents itself. Everything is perfect.

You are ALL. You are connected to the totality of that which exists, then what have you to fear?
Learn to love meeting yourself and listening to yourself.
Learn to deepen your self-knowledge.

Hierarchy is an illusion!
We all come from the same original Source. In truth, there is only 'You'.
You are the ONE. You come from the Great All.
So why do you give faith to this illusion which consists in considering yourself as inferior or superior to someone else? This isn't reality.

You are sovereign.
A child is the equal of his parent.
A king is the equal of his 'subject'.
A teacher is equal to the student.
A policeman is the equal of a citizen.
A cow is equal to its breeder.
A butterfly is equal to a mare.
We are the same entity.

You don't have to submit yourself to the requirements of a so-called superior.
You must not submit someone to your orders either. Nor to manipulate him to obey you.
You think, therefore you are.

And if you are, you exist. You are 'worth' the same as another being. No more and no less.

Hierarchy is an answer to the rule of duality which advocates opposites: high/low, rich/poor, good/mean, powerful/weak, decider/executor…
But on your way to Homo Deus, you don't believe in this duality anymore, which separates rather than unites.
Each day and in every area, you tend to incarnate Unity in physical matter.
Thus, your thoughts as your acts manifest this Unity, in total equity.

All hierarchy is pyramidal (vertical) whereas you are following the path of absolute horizontality where each person has his place and is worth the same.

Release yourself from the need of having to be assimilated to a group, to a village, a family or a couple.
Be free from your need to be alone.
Liberation of you habit to be always
in somebody's presence to justify your value
or to flee from your fears.
Be free from your belief that a person alone
is rejected, sad, unlikeable or unworthy of interest
and abandoned by his own.
YOU ARE EVERYTHING.

STEP 38

You are all.

You are the drop rejoining the ocean.
In fact, you are the ocean, which thinks to be a drop of water. Because you never have been separated from this ocean. You look like a drop that is alone and abandoned but it is an illusion.

Look around you. Imagine that the air around you is filled with a colored substance. This substance touches you but also the ground, the trees, the passersby, cars, houses, the bird or the plane passing above the clouds.
This same substance also encompasses the Earth, the Moon and the Sun. It even goes beyond our solar system.
It touches everything and everybody at the same time.
It has no limit. It circles around you as it circles every element of the galaxy. In our universe and different multiverses.
This emptiness is in contact with the whole that composes the Omniverse, and of you therefore!

With global warming caused by an acceleration of the Earth's vibration (and to the heightening temperature of the Sun), you can easily experiment the sensation of being united to the Great All. Because the heat helps you feel that your body has no more limit and is dilating…
The air around you is at the same temperature than your body and you seem to be losing your usual consistency!

When you are cold, it makes you shudder and tighten your arms around you. You feel that you are being aggressed by the exterior. The freshness of air helps to become conscious of your bodily contour.
This rising temperature makes us understand this universal tie, this connection with All.
Thus, you easily conceive that everything is connected. We are all interconnected.
This is wonderful news because it induces the fact that each thing you lay your conscience on will have an impact on the rest of the universe!
Yes! That which you live each day affects the whole of humanity.
Therefore, you must not wait for others to modify their behavior before starting to proceed to your own change.
Start now, even if you are sure that you are the only one.
The world is you.

The elite in power wants to have us believe that we are responsible for the climate imbalance so that we feel guilty and afraid of the upcoming ecological change.
Meanwhile, the governments offer to 'protect' us in exchange of increasingly freedom restricting laws, of tiring work and soon, of a chip to control and observe us…
This caste which conceives the enslavement of humanity to serve its own interests, is not there to bring this plan to pass. No.
In an absolute sense and in spite of the elite, its purpose is to push us onwards to our Homo Deus transformation.
It is thanks to that if we are led to evolve beyond the stage of Homo Sapiens to give the day to our divine version.

Without these ploys to organize human slavery, we would still be some brave and obeying 'sheep' unaware of their true nature.

Therefore, let us sincerely be thankful of this providential elite for the ingrate task they have accepted to do to ensure our evolution.

Remember: there is neither executor nor victim. Everything is perfect and we are ONE.

Consequently, you are them. And they are you.

The truth is that your soul has personally orchestrated their presence and despotic objectives in order to allow for your ascension to a superior stage.

Practice each day the Ho'oponopono technique towards them:

Dear elite, I am sorry.
Forgive me.
Thank you. I Love you.

Accomplish the modifications, which you feel to be important to you as soon as you get the profound conviction of it.

Improve your thoughts, words and actions as soon as you can.

Your Spirit wasn't created on your day of birth. Your soul comes from the All and will return to it after your physical death. To be more exact, you never did leave this All!

You have just forgotten that this is what you were during your incarnation(s).

Don't be afraid of death nor of the unknown that it represents because if there is a life after death, then there is one also before your birth and in all eternity.

Unconsciously, you know where you come from. This deep knowledge allows your spirit to be always at peace.
On the other hand, your ego/mindset knows very well that it is itself illusory, mortal and temporary.
It knows that it is going to disappear! This is what makes it be in a hurry, stressed, impatient, fearful. It is afraid of facing an inevitable nothingness.
Your soul is continually bathing in absolute quietude.
Try to appease your mind in order to connect to your essence. Thus, the great wisdom of Universal Love will guide you and you will cease to blindly follow the anguished advice of your ignorant ego.

To assimilate the realization of 'I am all' you are going to spend some time identifying yourself to what you see and hear. As a result, you are going to un-identify yourself from the human that you believe to be physically.

For example:
*"**I am this chair**. I am the Sun. I am this cat. I am the neighbor. I am my spouse. I am my son. I am your grandmother.*
But also, I am Trump. I am Mussolini. I am Hitler. I am the abbey Pierre. I am Gandhi. I am Buddha..."

Practice taking the place of others, of animals, plants and minerals.
By the same token, this exercise will avoid you losing your energy pondering over such thought, souvenir, remorse, regret or other niceties from the ego and mind.

"Know yourself and you will know the universe and the Gods."
Inscription on the Temple of Delphes.

Thus, I am the universe and I am the Gods.
Thus, so are you.

**Freedom from your habit to compare,
measure yourself to other human beings,
to animals, plants and minerals.
Release from the need of being superior or inferior
with respect to someone or to something else.
Liberation from your belief of being separated
from the rest of the world.
YOU ARE EVERYTHING.**

STEP 39

**Getting fed only with prana.
Then you will cease all food
and drink because you are ALL.
No solid food, no thick juice,
no diluted juice, no water.
And soon, not even prana.**

You don't need to eat or to drink because you are All.
You have totally integrated and are conscious of the fact that you are not this earthly being made of flesh and bone.
This physical body only represents one of your 'vehicles of matter', an avatar to live your existence on this planet.
But you are not 'in' this body. You are not only in this body since you are all and everywhere.
There is only You, since there is just one thing:
Absolute Conscience, the Great All, the Universal Source!
This omnipresent Source has played the game of forgetting itself to be able to discover and explore its innumerable facets.
The illusion of this three dimensional world has no more effect on you. You nourish yourself directly of the Love that you are. Because you are Love, you are ALL.
The fact of having to feed oneself is also an illusion since you are not this body, it doesn't really exist.

Before definitely ceasing to eat by conscientiously knowing that only Love exists, you can pass through the stage of pranic nourishment.

Which is to say to feed yourself on the energy around you and inside you. This energy is called prana.
Important reminder, it is not fasting but a way of how to be nourished from All!
The body is still being 'fed'.
The difference lies in the fact that instead of eating visible and dense food, your body gets nourished by the prana, the Qi, the energy, the highest vibration.
Everything is vibration.
Physical matter is energy that has been agglutinated, amalgamated, made denser.

If you ask yourself the question: "Pranic? I don't believe in it because there are people who are dying of hunger…"
Then I would answer that their beliefs create their reality.
Thus if you are convinced that you cannot live without food or drink, then you will die.
And if you are perfectly conscious that everything is an illusion and that your incarnate person is pure energy of Love, then you will live in excellent health without having to eat.
Each person generates his own reality according to his thoughts, his limiting beliefs, his words and his actions.
Now all these 'realities' are truths coexisting at the same moment.

Stay alert because this step is neither trivial nor to be taken lightly.
Keep on listening to your body.
Don't impose on yourself a pranic diet if you didn't train progressively to do so. Everything can be learnt but a good

amount of time, patience and perseverance will be necessary.

The lightening of your food, step by step, as suggested throughout this book, is ideal to attain that objective. Because it is something that is done gradually.

Quit following this diet if you become too thin and if your body weight is steadily decreasing without stabilizing itself. In this case, your body is informing you that you are not yet ready to pass this ultimate stage of conscience.

Accept what is, without expectation, without judgment.

Follow the call of your heart and respect the signals of your body.

Don't force anything, be flexible with yourself. Always love yourself.

Going to a pranic diet is an important and difficult change. Inform yourself by reading books on the subject before engaging yourself on this singular path.

If you have the least doubt on the impossibility of living exclusively on prana, then don't follow this path yet, your thoughts and beliefs are influencing your reality.

As Henry Ford said:

"Whether you think that you are capable or not capable, in both cases, you are right".

Now that you have become pranic, you don't sleep very much because your need to sleep is reduced to a minimum.

But also, you feel continually a powerful energy and a great vigor, because you are no longer parasited by the organic work of digestion or hunger pangs in your stomach.

You radiate from the inside and this 'light' propagates itself around you. Each being that you cross, each person with whom you speak or every place you pass through, is benefiting now of your high vibrations of joy and Love. You diffuse what you are.

By progressively listening to your body and intuition, you have freed yourself of having to ingest physical food.

You become conscious when you eat that it is the energy of the plant which feeds you and not the plant itself. Thus you conceive yourself being All and that All being energy, you are constantly fed in an ideal fashion, with or without prana.

We may assume that at this stage you are already on liquid-only and that the fact of eating doesn't concern you so much. You are already practically released from this function and constraint.

Follow your ideas naturally. Concentrate as soon as you can and listen to the needs of your physical body.

In order to check if your body has passed without difficulty to this new mode of nourishment, here are three criteria:

First, you are in excellent shape, full of energy and vitality. Next, you hardly ever sleep (perhaps 20 hours a week) and last, your body weight has ceased to decrease, it has stabilized.

If you feel the calling to adopt a pranic mode but that you would like to be accompanied during this transition, there are many workshops animated by pranic people in France and elsewhere.

These workshops are perfect to insure a serene guided transition, and allow you to meet other participants who are on the same evolutionary path as you.

When you will have become pranic, you will be able to pass on to the ultimate step: total freedom from all needs by being conscious that you have no need to be filled because everything is already there, everything is already accomplished.
The day will come when you won't need to breathe, nor even to die.
At that moment, you will have completely revealed your true nature beyond the illusory filter of your carnal body.
You will have become a Homo Deus, the next step of humanity.

Here are the names of many people who became pranic:

Prahlad Jani passed over seventy years without water nor food.
Ray Maor, Isabelle Hercelin, Dominique Verga, Lara Luce, Elitom El-amin, Adrienn Light, Dainius Mykolaitis, Choranti, Pascal Martelli and Gabriel Lesquoy (with whom I have personally done a prana workshop for two weeks).
Ram Bahadur Bomjon also named 'Buddha Boy' remained seated day and night in meditation under a tree for six years, without eating or drinking.
Angela Bittl had her first pranic experience at fifteen.

Alyna Rouelle, at eighteen years old, passed a month without eating or drinking in a state of absolute bliss. She then deepened her experience of pranic food during several years.
Edgardo Bonazzi is pranic since 2017. Kay Hougaard, since 2012. Christina Eltrayan is pranic since 2010.
Darell Brann practices Sun Gazing (feeding oneself only with sunlight). He has lived six months in the desert, practicing Sun Gazing from sunrise to dawn.
Dmitry Lapshinov (Dima) is nourished by prana since 2011.
Domenico Provenzano is pranic since 2010. Erika Witthuhn since 2001.
Fabrice De Graef was a raw vegetable and fruit eater for twenty years and passed to pranic food naturally during a visit to India.
Galina El-Sharas lives of prana since 2009.
Mira Omerzel (Mirit) lives of prana since 2000.
Monica Kunovska, since 2015, Nicolas Pilartz since 2012, Rishi Royal since 2002, Robert Ganski since 2015, Veni Loveandlight since 2004, Victor Truviano since 2010.
Nassim Haramein, a Swiss scientific physicist, has started experimenting with pranic food. He is among the lecturers at 'Pranic World Festival'.

You could watch the documentary *"Light"* by Peter-Arthur Straubinger.
Or also the film *"How to become a goddess. Living on love and fresh water"* about Dominique Verga.
She explains that since she has become pranic, eating a fruit is like eating an object like paper or cardboard.

She left the world of survival in which if she didn't eat or drink, she could die, to enter fully in the world of LIFE in which nothing can happen to her because she has no more needs. A world of LIFE in which she is permanently in a state of grace.

**You are free from your need to eat material,
solid or liquid food, because you are conscious
that everything is only vibration.
You decide to feed yourself of energy itself,
without passing by a plant or a liquid
having stored and assimilated it before.
You are released from your need to sleep,
which has become practically non-existent.
YOU ARE EVERYTHING.**

STEP 40

Everything is perfect.
Let go.

Now you have become the divine version of your present incarnation.
Welcome this state.
Live it in full conscience, at each moment of this existence.
On the other hand, if you haven't yet arrived, abandon this wish for the moment. Remember to avoid all inner conflict.

Let go of your expectations, your goals, your wants and hopes.
Cease all struggles.
Accept what is without judgment or guilt.
Accept yourself as you are.
Love yourself. Because loving yourself is to be in Unconditional Love towards yourself.
Are you what you wish to be? Never mind.
Did you succeed in doing what you had planned to do? It doesn't matter.
Just be who you are, as you are, when you are.
Because everything is perfect and you are EVERYTHING.

Keep these forty steps in mind. Re-read them regularly to impregnate again and again your flesh, subtle bodies and spirit.

You are neither an 'I' nor a personality that is apart from the rest of humanity. You are ONE.
You don't need a first name, a name, a spouse, a child, a friend, a family, a colleague, a co-citizen, an animal pet…
You don't need to eat, to drink or to sleep.
A day will come when even death will be a mirage in this three dimensional world.
Yes, physical immortality is the final stage of the Homo Deus that we are all called to incarnate. You will not become 'immortal', you will have simply completely integrated the fact that this existence is an allurement. You are outside of time. Therefore you are neither born nor dead. You just are.
This last veil will drop when you will have anchored on a daily basis your unified version of All. The Law of Attraction brings about a reality which suits your beliefs. Because your conscience is the origin of matter. Thus it creates the universe, your universe.

You no longer have any needs. You have no more fear.
Fear and needs disappear as soon as you remember that you are Unconditional Love and that you are experimenting a theater play in which all the actors are from a unique source, a unique raw material: this vibration of Love.
There doesn't exist anything else but this omnipresent breath of love.

It has engendered everything and continually creates everything. Nonetheless, it has never changed by a iota…
All paradoxes are possible in this world of illusion.

YOU ARE.
YOU ARE ONE.
If you have not been yet able to impregnate this truth in each of your physical cells, it's perfect as well. Because time is a mirage and, in spite of appearances, everything is already accomplished.
Even if you don't see it yet because the veil of habits is still present on you.

So, follow the road towards the luminous sun that you are. Continue on this magnificent path!
You have already succeeded. Because everything is experience. Failure doesn't exist since there is always a learning that takes place, an evolution of conscience thanks to our actions, whether they be 'successful' or a flop.
Everything is learning.
The path that is employed is as bright as the place you are supposed to arrive.

Re-read and integrate each of the forty steps leading to your Homo Deus state.
Love yourself, love others, love your enemies, love what makes you fearful, love what surrounds you. LOVE.
Treat everything and everyone with respect and kindness. Yourself included.

You have integrated that the plants are you. Animals too are you...
Treat all the 'you' with Unconditional Love.
Cherish all. Preserve everything.
Because all is Love. Because you are Love.

In order to remain constantly impregnated by your yearning to mute towards a Homo Deus state, I invite you to inform yourself on 'Personal sovereignty' in other words: Personocratia.

The author Ghis, has written many books to incarnate this state in all areas of daily living.
Since we live in a dictatorship disguised in democracy, Personocratia is the only way to live in this collectivity, by being connected to our individual conscience.
Her booklets denounce and show, among other things, the false democracy in which the world actually survives.
They are a precious tool to see beyond this indoctrination of the masses.

The entire universe is vibration.
Nikola Tesla was an inventor and engineer considered as one of the greatest scientists in the history of technology.
He worked in close partnership with Thomas Edison (inventor of electricity).
This is what he said:
"If you want to find the secrets of the universe, think in terms of energy, frequency and vibration."

**Freedom from your last expectations about yourself,
on your ability to incarnate the great person
that you already are.
Release from your last need which is to attain
the Homo Deus state and to evolve towards
the ideal being that you would like to be.
Everything is already accomplished.
YOU ARE EVERYTHING.**

"*From Homo Sapiens to Homo Deus*"
takes up the teachings from the book
"*How to become a Christ : A method in 40 days*".

SUMMARY:

STEP 1 — The unique unwavering certainty is that your conscience exists.

STEP 2 — Look at yourself lovingly. Love yourself.

STEP 3 — Become a vegetarian.

STEP 4 — Walk and particularly, walk in nature!

STEP 5 — Laugh and be joyful.

STEP 6 — Detach yourself from your roles and affiliations.

STEP 7 — What makes you suffer from the outside comes from pain inside of you.

STEP 8 — Don't identify yourself to the emotions you feel.

STEP 9 — You no longer need to think about the past.

STEP 10 — You no longer need to worry about the future.

STEP 11 — Become a vegan.

STEP 12 — Drink some water, more water and still more water.

STEP 13 — Live and act in the PRESENT!

STEP 14 — Free-will is an illusion.

STEP 15 — 'Unity' or 'Duality'.

STEP 16 — Let go of your expectations, your desires, your hopes.

STEP 17 — Let go of all your fears.

STEP 18 — Adopt a raw diet.

STEP 19 — You are complete.

STEP 20 — Go on a liquid diet.

STEP 21 — You're on earth to evolve from inside.

STEP 22 — You are immortal.

STEP 23 — You heal yourself.

STEP 24 — Create a world of truth.

STEP 25 — You are ageless.

STEP 26 — The illusion of the couple.

STEP 27 — You don't 'need' anything anymore to be happy and joyful.

STEP 28 — Cease all struggle within you.

STEP 29 — Cease all judgment.

STEP 30 — Become a breatharian. Drink water, fruit juices without pulp, vegetable broths without any solids in suspension.

STEP 31 — You are no longer sad for people that you have lost, whether they be dead or still alive.

STEP 32 — In this world of illusion, everything is in perpetual movement. On the other hand, in Reality, nothing ever changes.

STEP 33 — Only Love exists.

STEP 34 — About forgiveness.

STEP 35 — Transcend your ego.

STEP 36 — The importance of silence and of all the answers it contains.

STEP 37 — Solitude! Forty days in the desert, alone, face to face with oneself.

STEP 38 — You are all.

STEP 39 — Getting fed only with prana. Then you will cease all food and drink because you are ALL.

STEP 40 — Everything is perfect. Let go.

Bibliography et websites :

– « *The Hidden Messages in Water*», Maseru Emoto.
– « *Living on Light - The Source of Nourishment for the New Millennium*», Jasmuheen.
– « *La nutri-émotion* », Nassrine Reza.
– « *Power To Bloom*», Nassrine Reza.
– « *Vous êtes votre propre guide* », Nassrine Reza.
– « *La nutrition de la liberté* », Alyna Rouelle.
– « *Urinothérapie* », Dr Christian Tal Schaller et Johanne Razanamahay.
– « *What The Hell Am I Doing Here Anyway?*» Ghislaine Saint-Pierre Lanctôt.
– Les 10 « *Livrets de Personocratia* », propos de Ghis recueillis et rédigés par Mado.
– « *Et si on s'arrêtait un peu de manger... de temps en temps* », Bernard Clavière.
– « *L'éveil de la rose* », Pascale Leconte.
– « *Opening Doors Within: 365 Daily Meditations from Findhorn* », Eileen Caddy.
– « *Les pervers narcissiques* », Jean-Charles Bouchoux.
– « *Nonviolent Communication: A Language of Life* », Marshall B. Rosenberg.
– « *Les modes d'emploi de Lulumineuse* », Lulumineuse.
– « *Hi-ya, Me Love! Human User Guide* », Lulumineuse and Art-Mella.
– « *De la Nourriture Prânique à la Plénitude du Vide.* », Gabriel Lesquoy.
– « *How to become a Christ : Method in 40 days*», Toi Tout.
– « *Being Genuine: Stop Being Nice, Start Being Real* », Thomas d'Ansembourg.
– « *Heal your wounds & find your true self* », Lise Bourbeau.
– « *The secret* », Rhonda Byrne.
– « *Life from Light: Is it Possible to Live without Food? - A Scientist Reports on His Experiences*», Michael Werner.